a journey with Jonah to

Find God's Will For You

James D. Devine

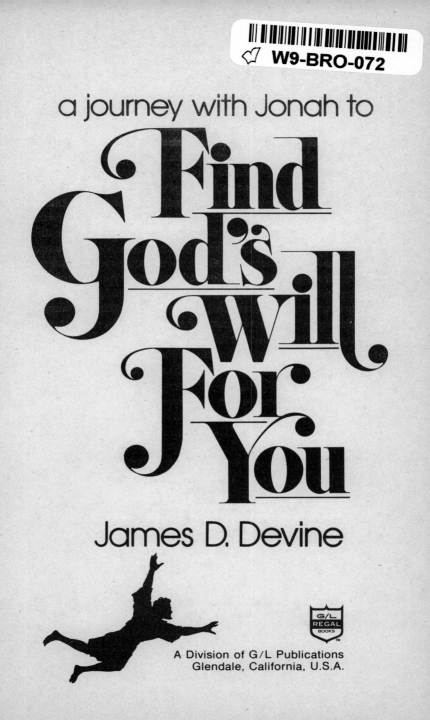

G/L REGAL BOOKS™

A Division of G/L Publications
Glendale, California, U.S.A.

Dedicated to my
lovely wife,
LYNN,
who by the grace of God
and in her own unique way
is discipling me
into a useful servant
of the Lord Jesus Christ.

Scripture quotations in this publication, unless
otherwise indicated, are from the *NASB, New American
Standard Bible.* © The Lockman Foundation 1960, 1962,
1963, 1968, 1971. Used by permission.
Other versions are *KJV, King James Version*
Phillips, The New Testament in Modern English, Revised
Edition, J.B. Phillips 1958, 1960, 1972. Used by
permission of Macmillan Publishing Co., Inc.

Published by Regal Books Division, G/L Publications
Glendale, California 91209,
Printed in U.S.A.

Library of Congress Catalog Card No. 76-57035
ISBN 0-8307-0527-9

Contents

Preface

Swallow a mouthful of saltwater and you'll never forget the taste! Jonah did this and the experience made a lasting impression in his life. In fact, he went through a number of situations that you can easily identify with in your life. Have you ever felt discouraged or angry; have you ever wanted to throw in the towel? These are common human experiences, and Jonah was captured by each of them.

Come with me into these four brief chapters from the Bible and get ready for a very human but exciting drama! Keep an open Bible handy as you read along. Begin to put yourself into Jonah's sandals; think and feel with him as he relates his intriguing story. Taste the salty Mediterranean with your keen imagination, and let the shivers run up and down your spine as the prophet is tossed into the blue. Sense the darkness and horror of a fish's belly. Above everything else, get ready to encounter the grace and power of a great God!

These messages were first preached at Powellhurst Baptist Church in Portland, Oregon, from September to December of 1975. God used the power of His Word to speak to our hearts in a wonderful way. I want you to experience for yourself the tremendous practicality of this brief narrative.

I wish to express my deep gratitude to the family of Powellhurst Baptist Church. As their young pastor I have received generous and encouraging compliments as well as gentle and effective corrections. This balance has both challenged me and caused me to grow in my relationship with the Lord Jesus during this first year of pastoral ministry.

I am also indebted to four faculty members at Western Conservative Baptist Seminary: Dr. Stanley Ellisen for teaching me the importance of a synthetic view of God's Word; Dr. Grant Howard for his loving and stimulating motivation; Dr. Ralph Alexander for his practical insights into the book of Jonah in Hebrew 104; and Prof. "Mike" Jones for his creative encouragement in homiletics.

Without a dedicated staff of secretarial help this book would not have become a reality. My sincere appreciation to a great team—Patti Rogers, Dorothy Chester, Esther Keosababian, Joyce Payne, and Joy Hatch!

Parents play such a unique role in the lives of their children. My love and praise is deeply expressed to my dad for his demonstration of the tender and patient love of a father who really cares. To my creative and enthusiastic mother I acknowledge my great interest in dynamic expression and sensitivity to people's needs.

And to my own precious gang of Lynn, Matthew, Shelly, and Daniel, I want to express what cannot be adequately formulated. The joy and responsibility I have in sharing the love of Jesus with you is my highest calling!

1 | Introduction to a Fascinating Journey

Each evening several hundred cars waited their turn to push through the gates of the drive-in theater. The drivers jockeyed for position, eagerly anticipating those breathtaking moments displayed on the towering screen. From the opening scenes their attention was gripped by the entertainment smash of all time: *Jaws!*

How did author Peter Benchley know? After he penned his best-selling novel *Jaws*, the creative juices of Hollywood's best talent began to flow with ideas for the movie production. The theme of the book would prove captivating to the cinematic tastebuds of millions of viewers: "The great fish moved silently through the night water, propelled by short sweeps of its crescent tail."

Every major city in the United States was hit with an epidemic of *Jaws* fever." The movie production of this longest-running best-seller grossed $124.3 million in its first 78 days after release! The movie is bloody and suspenseful, and it is swept along by highly dramatic scenes. The central focus of attention is a gigantic white shark whose habit of devouring innocent swimmers terrorizes a resort community.

For a while everyone was captivated. Your local butcher would tell you that it was temporarily impossible to buy shark's meat. Shortly after the film's debut my son pointed out a gruesome-looking hulk of a shark's head painted brilliantly on a $2.66 T-shirt at our local K-Mart discount store! Wherever you turned, Jaws stood ready, with shining rows of spiked teeth, to bite your head off! One local jeweler slipped a 24-karat gold chain through a shark's tooth and boldly advertised, "Here is the shark's devastating weapon against man and nature . . . wear it . . . feel the strength of the shark . . . !" It is amazing how three mechanically designed metal animals (created by a retired specialist from Walt Disney Productions for the tidy sum of $225,000) could grip the attention of an entire nation!

When we open our Bibles and turn to the book of Jonah, we are not dazzled by the brilliance of Hollywood but by the radiance of the glory of God. Though Jonah has not enjoyed as sophisticated a publicity campaign as *Jaws*, it contains a far greater drama than this twentieth-century production. It's not just another whale story!

Jonah's four brief chapters usually cover only one or two pages of any particular Bible, but this brief book has been placed in Scripture for our instruction by the Spirit of God. We will study Jonah verse-by-verse in the following chapters, which are arranged as a biblical drama of history in 13 acts.

Why should we study such a short piece of writing that several critics have titled "The Greatest Fish Story of All Time," and which pagans have mocked and excluded from their own literature? I think there are two primary reasons that compel us to give Jonah our undivided attention.

The Love and Mercy of God

How powerfully and graphically the all-inclusive love and mercy of God are displayed to the prophet Jonah! Men are too easily limited by their mundane sphere of life; they too readily forget the character of their Creator. As A.W. Tozer in *Knowledge of the Holy* has reminded us, we are desperately in need of a proper view of God *as He is*, and not *how we would like Him to be!*

This fact stunned me into some deep thinking as a self-sufficient, unanchored, uncommitted college student at the University of Washington. Mack Crenshaw, the speaker and director of the college ministry of Campus Crusade for Christ, gave a simple but spiritually eye-opening message on how we see God. Instead of knowing and understanding His divine character through the written revelation of Himself (the Bible), we choose to place a grid of muddled thinking and selfish reasoning over our minds, allowing only certain "good" things (those that benefit us and do not challenge our way of living) to filter through. But the real privilege is to learn of God's character and attributes through His Word.

Another attribute of God that we will see is His sovereign control over men and events. Does God care about me? Has He, as the critics blindly cry, wound up the universe like a top and left it to spin itself to a fumbling halt? From Jonah we learn that this notion never enters the mind of God. On the contrary, He has unreservedly committed Himself to man, His unique creation, and utilizes every possible means to bring rebellious men back to Himself.

The Reality of Human Nature

This book is certainly about God, but it also provides us with great insight about man. Jonah was a man just as we are. He was a prophet, yes, but he also struggled, groped, and agonized over the will of God for his life. We have a slice of reality here! You and I struggle with the same question: "What does God want *me* to do?"

Jonah was commissioned with an assignment that he just did not want to fulfill. Have you ever felt like that? God tells you to do something and your response is, "Really, Lord, you've got to be kidding!" By our words or unspoken internal attitudes we challenge God's direction in our lives.

Jonah not only struggled to obey the word and will of God, but he also displayed another common attitude—that of relying on his own insight. Jonah neglected the wisdom of Proverbs 3:5,6: "Trust in the Lord with all your heart, and do not lean on your own understanding. In all your ways acknowledge Him, and He will make your paths straight."

We can also identify with Jonah as he evidenced a love for the comfortable way of life. He was not about to grit his teeth for God and deliver any message of mercy to those unbelieving Gentiles in Nineveh! How much like Jonah we are! How often we seek to please God by thinking we can promenade down easy street in our Christian lives. We crave comfort, but

8

God craves *commitment*, no matter what the cost. His will is to develop the character of His Son in us, and that process is costly (Rom. 8:28,29; Phil. 1:29,30).

A Fresh Picture of God

Another attitude of man that Jonah evidences is perhaps the greatest: his urgent need to see a fresh picture of God. All too often we lose our appreciation for something or someone due to constant exposure. The homemaker's true appreciation of her new washing machine is at its height when her thoughtful husband brings it home as a surprise. She can remember all those trips down to the corner laundromat—rain or shine, week after week. But now, there stands her very own machine! Let's look in on this happy scene a few months later. The dirty clothes don't stop, but only seem to pile higher and higher. So out she goes to the garage once or twice a day. The *delight* is gone, and the routine *duty* has set in.

So it is with our wonderful God. We don't like to admit this, but it can be and often is the truth nevertheless. "This Christian life seems like a drag. What happened? When I first received the Lord Jesus Christ as my Saviour it was thrilling! But now it's different. What's the matter?"

Exposure? Yes, but the wrong kind. Instead of exposure that *revitalizes our faith*, we have experienced an exposure that has *rusted our joy*. The direction of the relationship has shifted from the *person of God* to the *opinions of people*. The truth Jonah needed to learn was that *men disappoint*, but *God develops*. If the focus of our attention is on men, then we can expect little joy in the Christian life. But if the focus of our attention is on our great God, with His unique attributes, then our joy will be developed.

Jonah needed a fresh picture of God. So do I. So do you!

Interpreting the Book of Jonah

One of the strongest evidences that the story of Jonah really happened in history comes from the lips of Jesus Christ Himself. In no less than three separate instances (Matt. 12:39-44; 16:1-4; Luke 11:29-32) our Lord pointed convincingly to the historical person of Jonah and the facts of his mission to the Ninevites. He even used Jonah's circumstances as a significant illustration for His own life and ministry.[1]

Several different methods of interpretation have been proposed for the book of Jonah. Among the more popular are the mythical, allegorical (parabolic), symbolic, historical, and predictive-typical-historical methods.[2]

In this study we will take the position that the book of Jonah is a straightforward historical work containing one instance of prediction (3:4) and intimations of symbolism of Christ throughout the book.[3] If we strip the book of its historical objectivity and its biographical insight, we immediately enter the dubious realm of allegory, legend, and parable. We must maintain the biblical premise that "all Scripture is inspired of God [that is, 'breathed out' from the mouth and mind of God Himself] and profitable for teaching, for reproof, for correction, for training in righteousness; that the man of God may be adequate, equipped for every good work" (2 Tim. 3:16,17; see also 1 Pet. 1:22-25; 2 Pet. 1:20,21). This Bible that has been entrusted to man is the very Word of God, infallible and inerrant in its entirety, our sole and final authority in all matters of faith and practice. We must certainly recognize the distinguishing elements of figures of speech and parabolic texts, but Jonah's objectivity cannot be classed in this area.

No Mere Allegory

Some of the critics favor an allegorical approach to the book. They would have us believe that the prophet Jonah is an allegorical figure who represents disobedient Israel and that the sea represents the Gentiles. They also throw in the "whale," which supposedly stands for the city of Babylon. Jonah's "vacation" in the belly of the great fish is a representation for the Babylonian captivity!

Other theories exist as well. Gleason Archer comments at this point: "A closer examination of the text, however, shows that numerous features of the narrative can scarcely be fitted into the allegorical pattern. If the whale represented Babylon, what did Nineveh represent? As for the ship that set sail from Joppa, it is hard to see what this would correspond with in the allegory, nor is it clear why three days should be selected to represent seventy years of captivity. Furthermore, there is not the slightest historical evidence to show the existence of any such universalistic sentiment among the fifth-century Jews as this theory predicates."[4]

Not only is the story of Jonah a true narrative or diary, but it contains in its brief pages several pictures (sometimes called "shadows" or "types"—Col. 2:17; Heb. 8:5; Rom. 5:14) of the person of our Saviour, especially in Jonah 1:17. This narrative also reveals to us in a general way something of the nation of Israel outside the land of promise (pictured by the prophet Jonah being in Gentile territory).[5] We should not try to make every detail a symbolic representation.

J. Vernon McGee lists several significant truths which we can gain from these four chapters: 1) they set forth the resurrection; 2) they teach us that salvation is not earned by works; 3) they reveal to us that God's purposes of grace cannot be frustrated and that He will not cast us aside for our faithlessness; and 4) they teach us that God's character is good and gracious—that He is the God of *all* men, even the Gentiles![6]

The general theme of the book of Jonah is that

GOD IS SOVEREIGN AND LOVES ALL PEOPLE.

Footnotes

1. Richard Chenevix Trench, *Synonyms of the New Testament* (Grand Rapids: Wm. B. Eerdmans, 1939), pp. 339ff. The word that Jesus used was "sign" (Greek, *sémeion*). This term was employed to describe the supernatural works wrought by Jesus Christ. The word points to the ethical purpose of Jesus' signs, and it highlights the grace and power of the doer. The signs pointed to Jesus' authoritative credentials as the Messiah, the Son of God.

2. For a discussion of several of the proposed methods of interpretation, see George L. Robinson, *The Twelve Minor Prophets* (Grand Rapids: Baker Book House, 1974), pp. 83-87.

3. Frank E. Gaebelein in *The Servant and the Dove* (New York: Our Hope Press, 1946), p. 137, says, "After all, the four chapters contain just one sentence of direct, spoken prophecy. That sentence, it will be recalled, is as follows: 'Yet forty days, and Nineveh shall be overthrown' (3:4, *KJV*)."

4. Gleason L. Archer, *A Survey of Old Testament Introduction* (Chicago: Moody Press, 1964), P. 297.

5. See Henrietta C. Mears, *What the Bible Is All About* (Glendale: Regal Books, 1953), p. 303, for a comparison between Jonah and the nation of Israel.

6. J. Vernon McGee, *Jonah* (Outline Notes), *Thru the Bible Radio*, n.d., pp. 271,272.

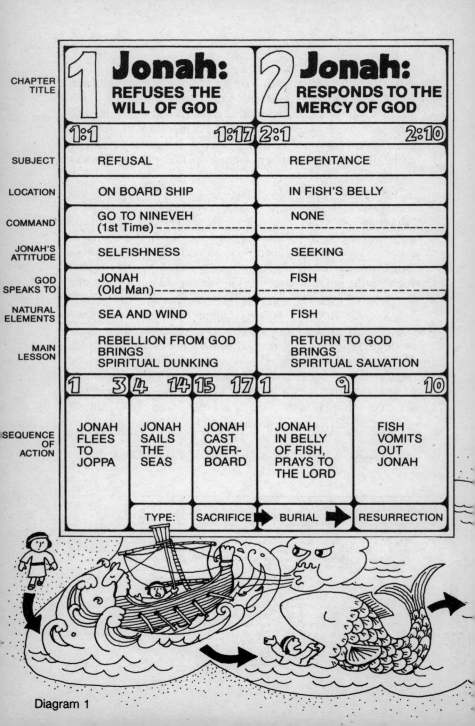

CHAPTER TITLE	**1** Jonah: REFUSES THE WILL OF GOD			**2** Jonah: RESPONDS TO THE MERCY OF GOD	
	1:1　　　　　　　1:17			2:1　　　　　　　2:10	
SUBJECT	REFUSAL			REPENTANCE	
LOCATION	ON BOARD SHIP			IN FISH'S BELLY	
COMMAND	GO TO NINEVEH (1st Time)--------------			NONE --------------------------	
JONAH'S ATTITUDE	SELFISHNESS			SEEKING	
GOD SPEAKS TO	JONAH (Old Man)--------------			FISH --------------------------	
NATURAL ELEMENTS	SEA AND WIND			FISH	
MAIN LESSON	REBELLION FROM GOD BRINGS SPIRITUAL DUNKING			RETURN TO GOD BRINGS SPIRITUAL SALVATION	
	1　　**3**	**4**　　**14**	**15**　　**17**	**1**　　　**9**	**10**
SEQUENCE OF ACTION	JONAH FLEES TO JOPPA	JONAH SAILS THE SEAS	JONAH CAST OVER-BOARD	JONAH IN BELLY OF FISH, PRAYS TO THE LORD	FISH VOMITS OUT JONAH
		TYPE:	SACRIFICE ➡	BURIAL ➡	RESURRECTION

Diagram 1

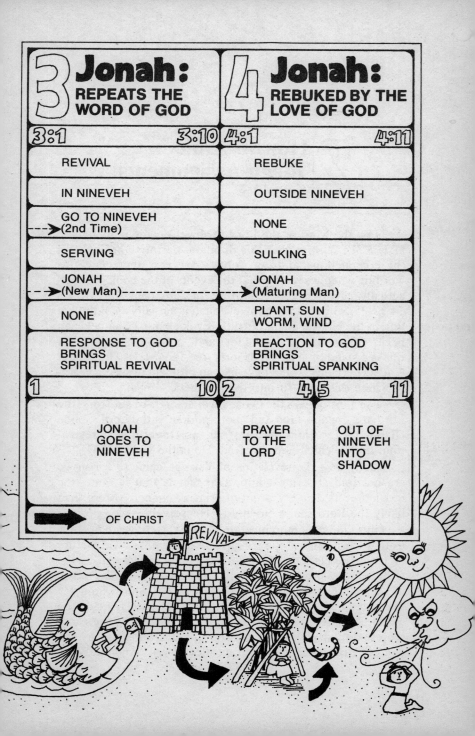

3 Jonah: REPEATS THE WORD OF GOD

3:1 ————————————— **3:10**

REVIVAL
IN NINEVEH
GO TO NINEVEH ---▶ (2nd Time)
SERVING
JONAH ---▶ (New Man) --------------- ▶
NONE
RESPONSE TO GOD BRINGS SPIRITUAL REVIVAL

1 ——————— **10** **2** ——— **4** **5** ——— **11**

JONAH GOES TO NINEVEH

➡ OF CHRIST

4 Jonah: REBUKED BY THE LOVE OF GOD

4:1 ————————————— **4:11**

REBUKE
OUTSIDE NINEVEH
NONE
SULKING
JONAH ▶ (Maturing Man)
PLANT, SUN WORM, WIND
REACTION TO GOD BRINGS SPIRITUAL SPANKING

PRAYER TO THE LORD	OUT OF NINEVEH INTO SHADOW

REVIVAL

2 | How to Avoid Tough Assignments!
Jonah 1:1–3

"Now the word of the Lord (Yahweh) came unto Jonah" (1:1, *KJV*). Notice that this dramatic narrative begins with the conjunction "and" or "now." We can appreciate this wording when we realize that the events of the book of Jonah actually occurred about the time of Jeroboam II (2 Kings 14:23-25), and that the book of Jonah is actually a continuing link in the biblical chain of truth. Ezekiel and 1 Samuel each begin with the Hebrew word for "and" or "now"; we find that this is a standing formula of sorts (see Judg. 1:1). The Jewish readers certainly would have had no problem in seeing exactly where this book fit into the prophetic stream.

Verse 1 introduces the two main characters of our story, the Lord and Jonah—God and man. *Yahweh* is the Lord's name (Exod. 3:9-18). He is the Designer and Director of all revelation, the covenant-keeping God; He is the great I AM.

Exactly *how* the revelation of Yahweh came to Jonah we are not told. The most important fact is that it came; the method of its delivery is not of primary concern. More than likely the Lord spoke directly to His servant.

Is this kind of communication unusual? Hebrews 1:1-3 tells us that Christians of our era have an even more vivid picture of God's revelation: "God, after He spoke long ago to the fathers in the prophets in many portions and in many ways, in these last days has spoken to us in His Son, whom He appointed heir of all things, through whom also He made the world. And He is the radiance of His glory and the exact representation of His nature, and upholds all things by the word of His power." John the apostle tells us, "And the Word

14

became flesh, and dwelt [literally 'tented'] among us, and we beheld His glory, glory as of the only begotten from the Father, full of grace and truth" (John 1:14). Jesus Christ is the supreme revelation of God the Father.

The Background Facts

Jonah was a prophet to the Northern Kingdom of Israel during the days of Jeroboam II (793-753 B.C.). You might say that this was the "golden era" of prosperity for Israel. Under Jeroboam's political and military leadership the geographical boundaries of Israel were extended to include all the territory gained earlier by King David and King Solomon.

This was a beautiful, prosperous time for Israel. It would be very easy for the people to say to themselves, "Now we really have a king who has put it all together!" Jonah must have been rather special, since it was he who had predicted that the nation would blossom and flourish (2 Kings 14:25).

The time of Jonah's ministry to the Northern Kingdom of Israel was 775-750 B.C. The prophets Amos (750 B.C.) and Hosea (755-725 B.C.) also had significant ministries to Israel. The kingdom had been earlier divided in 931 B.C.—Judah to the south and Israel to the north.

Jonah's hometown was Gath-hepher in Zebulon, about four miles north of Nazareth. Nearly 750 years later there was to be another Prophet associated with this little country spot of Nazareth. It was here that Jesus Christ, in willing obedience to His family, would grow up and "[increase] in wisdom and stature, and in favor with God and men" (Luke 2:51,52).

The word of the Lord came to Jonah probably in the latter years of his life. Some have called Jonah the first "foreign missionary" or the first "apostle to the Gentiles." What did God have in mind for this man? Was Jonah ready for God's command? Jonah needed to learn that *the will of God may not always be what you like, but it is always right.*

Jonah and the Will of God

Let's examine the command of the Lord that came to the "dove," the son of Amittai: "Arise, go to Nineveh" (1:2).

Looking ahead to Jonah's response in verse 3, I'll bet he closed his ears after these four short words! Though it is not recorded in our text, we can well imagine what began to swirl in Jonah's mind. If he really would have told God his thoughts at that very moment, they probably would have sounded something like this:

Lord: "Arise!"

Jonah: "Okay, Lord, I'm reading you loud and clear!"

Lord: " ... go ... "

Jonah: "Right, God. I'm on my way!"

Lord: " ... to Nineveh."

Jonah: "Did I hear you right? You're kidding, aren't you? (Silence.) You mean I'm supposed to travel over 500 miles from my homeland and go to that unbelieving nation of wild, violent people and preach against them? What kind of assignment is *this*, Lord? You've never directed me like this before!

"Yes, I know about them! But God, I'm a country man, not a city person! I'm a good patriot. What if some of my people see me doing this? I'll lose all my prophet's status! Please, isn't there another prophet around here you can send?"

Though Jonah didn't say these exact words, he could have been pondering thoughts similar to these.

Are you in the habit of being a grumbler in the face of God's leading in your life? Remember, God does not disappoint; He develops. The Lord's personal purposes for Jonah's life are the same as those for your life: to develop the character of Jesus Christ in you (Rom. 8:29). His intent is not to lead us into situations in which He gets some sort of sadistic thrill over our agony, pain, and frustration. Instead, "God causes all things to work together for good" (Rom. 8:28). He has committed Himself solely to holy purposes, and these have their source in His holy character (Isa. 6:3).

The Wicked City

Nineveh is described as a "great city." It was founded by Nimrod (Gen. 10:11) and had become the capital of the Assyrian Empire. The name Nineveh was used in a dual sense:

for the city proper and for the trapezoidal four-city complex that measured about 12 miles in circumference.

Fortified walls, perhaps as much as 100 feet high and 50 feet thick, surrounded this gigantic, sprawling metropolis on the eastern banks of the Tigris River. Nineveh was known as an ancient city-state, mammoth in size. From an indication in Jonah 4:11 that Nineveh had 120,000 infants, we may surmise (together with our knowledge of the archaeological data) that the city contained a population of at least 600,000 people. It was the largest city in the world at this time. That makes quite a congregation for any preacher!

From an inscription on a monument of King Ashurnasipal II we learn that 70,000 of Nineveh's elite society attended the dedication banquet at the king's palace. Critics of biblical history were silenced by this discovery that supported the evidence for Nineveh's large population.[1]

The Lord's statement of Nineveh's greatness most certainly referred to the fact that this Gentile concentration of thousands was going to play a great role in His merciful design. True greatness would come with a proper relationship to Yahweh; the city would be great for the sake of God's name.

The Lone Voice

What was one prophet to do in the midst of such a city? "Cry against it." This same word in Hebrew has its counterpart in Greek and literally means "to preach, to call out." Jonah was to be God's ambassador of warning to the enemies of Israel. He was to preach the very Word of God!

But Jonah wasn't in any mood to do this! His opinion was that the Ninevites should continue in their sinful ways, so that the Lord would suddenly extinguish the whole city! In this way their threat against Israel would be averted. "Why go, Lord? The journey is so long. Can't you find someone else?" Jonah continued to balk at his calling.

But God's word continues: "For their wickedness has come up before me." This same word for wickedness was used in reference to Cain (Gen. 4:10) and Sodom (Gen. 18:20,21). What it referred to was the people's tendency to do evil toward one another—in other words, their sins of violence (cf. Jon. 3:8) and treachery rather than the whole gamut of human sins and corruption.

The preaching prophet was being sent into dangerously hostile territory. In some of our churches this kind of environment is not so unusual. If sin is allowed to continue without proper, biblical discipline, the pastor may find himself in unfriendly surroundings. Impossible, you say? I wonder how often our own wickedness comes up before the Father—sin left to fester and decay. Our polite response is to think that by prayer ("Let's share this at the Wednesday night prayer meeting") and by subtle hints we can deal with the problem. But God sent Jonah directly into the eye of the hurricane to boldly send the light of His truth into the darkness of sin.

Have you ever received an assignment like this? As a child of God you discern that God is definitely leading you by the harmonious combination of His written Word, the leading of His Spirit, and His designed circumstances. His will is made clear to you. You are to do something that is just "not your bag," so you say to the Lord: "You're not serious, are you, Lord? You really don't expect *me* to do *this*—!"

We begin just like Jonah. Rather than concentrating on the very word and will of God, clear and unmistakable, we shift our allegiance to our personal patriotism or our personal prestige. Our greatest concern is not with *pleasing God* but with *pleasing ourselves*. Proverbs 29:25 cautions us against this alternative: "The fear of man brings a snare, but he who trusts in the Lord will be exalted." *The will of God may not always be what you like, but it is always right.*

God and the Will of Jonah

What was going on in Jonah's heart and mind? Perhaps he was thinking of his own people. We learn from the statement in 4:2 that Jonah was fearful of what God would do, because he knew that God was faithful. This sounds reasonable, but why do we read in verse 3 of Jonah's actions that ran counter to this conviction? "But Jonah rose up to flee to Tarshish from the presence of the Lord."

18

He heard the Lord's word that clearly conveyed the Lord's will. Jonah arose, but he got up "to flee." That clause details for us that his response had an intended purpose of disobedience. The Lord tells Jonah to go east, but the prophet flees westward. In fact, Jonah's destination is about the farthest point west he could possibly go! Tarshish was a Phoenician seaport in Spain, near Gibraltar (see Gen. 10:4; Isa 23:1).

"Go east, young man."

"Sorry, Lord, I've got other plans on the West Coast!"

How do we explain this? Did Jonah fear those 600,000 inhabitants in that great, cruel city of Nineveh? Probably not. He no doubt had faced tough assignments before. He did not fear *the people*, nor did he shrink back from crying out against their wickedness. Jonah feared what *God* would do. He had walked with God long enough to know of His faithfulness, His love, and His mercy. Jonah had become accustomed to obeying God in reference to *his own people*, but he had no experience or desire to do God's work toward *those Gentiles!* He didn't want to share the message of God's mercy with them!

What if they repented? Perhaps Israel would lose her specific, honorable status of being God's covenant nation. "Lord, I don't want to extend your grace and love and mercy to *those* people! Look at them—they're not worth it, Lord."

Jonah was caught. His own selfish, nearsighted view of God consumed his thinking. Other prophets rose up to *obey*, but Jonah rose up to *disobey*. One lesson is clear: just by changing our environment we will not solve our problems!

The first words of verse 3 capture a very tragic moment. Jonah was no dumbbell. He seemed mature in most areas—until God spoke to his one weak area! The servant of God is asked to convey the mercy of God to an unlovely group of people. Do *we* stumble at this point?

An Open Heart?

One Saturday evening I was busily preparing a sermon on 1 John 3:17: "But whoever has the world's good, and beholds his brother in need and closes his heart against him, how does the love of God abide in him?" A light rain was falling outside.

19

Inside our warm and cozy home, Lynn had put Matthew to bed. While she was relaxing in the living room, I was typing my sermon in the study. This tranquil setting was rudely interrupted by the ringing of the telephone:

"Hello?"

"Yeah . . . is this the person who talked to me at the Union Gospel Mission last week? This is Ted."

"Ah . . . yes, Ted, this is Jim Devine. What's the problem?"

"Well, you said you'd be glad to help us when we needed something. I need some food and a place to stay. Will you come down right now?"

The next few moments seemed stretched out to hours! I had *just* finished typing the word "closes" in the phrase "and closes his heart against him." The word is very graphic. It signifies a "snapping shut" or "locking shut" as a gate or door of our inner feelings.

Ted's words haunted me! "You said you'd help . . . will you come down right now!" I felt a real pull inside. Why would I want to go downtown and leave my sophisticated and comfortable spot just to give a drunk some help? "He probably wants some additional money for booze." Thoughts of reneging on my promise raced through my mind.

Soon the director of the mission came on the line, and before we finished talking I was able to see that Ted was cared for. But during those anxious moments, especially having studied the very verse which exhorts us to extend the love of God in practical, life-related ways, I was challenged to manifest His love to an unlovely, sinful man. I failed within. My attitude was just like Jonah's: "Not me, Lord." My selfish concerns took precedence over another's needs. May God teach us to display the love of Jesus Christ unselfishly and unconditionally, especially to those within our local church fellowship!

The Futile Flight from God

Jonah rose up to flee to Tarshish "from the presence of the Lord." He was going to get away from being God's messenger. Though disobedient, Jonah was not ignorant of the truth

20

in the Psalms, especially David's words in Psalm 139:7,9,10: "Where can I go from Thy Spirit? Or where can I flee from Thy presence? ... If I take the wings of the dawn, if I dwell in the remotest part of the sea, even there Thy hand will lead me, and Thy right hand will lay hold of me."

He knew that escape from God was impossible. What he was *really* saying was this: "Lord, I give up. Someone else can take the job of being your prophet." Jonah ran from the responsibility God wanted him to fulfill. He wanted to remove himself as far as possible from Israel, and perhaps Tarshish would be a haven.

Let us not overlook Jonah's sensitivity to God. He *did* arise and go, but not according to what God had told him. His personal feelings for his own people got in the way. The psalmist says that "the fear of man brings a snare" (Prov. 29:25). We often discern God's leading, but disobey in carrying out His gracious will. We all tend to offer God such "good" excuses! "How about my good works, my civic contributions, my many accomplishments in the church?" So it was with Jonah.

Instead of *walking with God*, Jonah *ran from God*. Instead of *walking with God*, Jonah would soon end up *wallowing in the sea!*

"So he went down to Joppa, found a ship which was going to Tarshish, paid the fare, and went down into it to go with them to Tarshish from the presence of the Lord" (1:3).

Notice what happens to the person who flees from serving the Lord. Jonah steps *down* from his prophetic office, he goes *down* to the seaport harbor of Joppa (this is downhill geographically), [2] and he slips *down* into the ship. We will discover in verse 5 that Jonah goes *down* still further into this Phoenician vessel. His pathway is marked "down" in every respect!

What a break! The ship is just ready to leave, and it is headed for Jonah's very destination of Tarshish! The runaway pays the ship fare and climbs aboard. Jonah's shipmates are a ragged bunch of unbelieving, pagan mariners. He joins himself to those who do not know the Lord, who have never had

21

the Word of God, and who have never known the joys of true worship.

From one vantage point it appears that Jonah managed to do all right for himself. The ship was there, the money was paid, the destination was correct, and the motley group of sailors would serve as an excellent covering for his escape. Surely no one would spot an ex-prophet in this gang of men! What started out as a rebellious flight from the presence of the Lord now *seems* to be turning out to Jonah's advantage. His circumstances are fitting together like a hand in a glove (see Ps. 107:23-32).

Circumstances and the Will of God

Are you struggling to realize the will of God for your life? Here is a very important lesson, taught by Jonah in flight from God: *Circumstances alone are not an adequate indication for knowing the will of God for your life.* God will never contradict His Word, even if for a short while it appears that disobedience pays.

At this time Jonah was probably feeling somewhat surprised, and perhaps even a bit cocky. His focus of trust was now directed toward the events before him. How shallow is this kind of faith! The fearful prophet was concerned with only *one aspect* of discerning the Lord's will; he had run from the other two aspects—the Word of God and the direction of the Spirit of God.

Circumstances must always be in harmony with the Word of God and the leading of the Spirit of God. Don't sell yourself short on circumstances alone, even if they appear to be tailor-made.

However convenient his circumstances, Jonah was not really concerned about knowing the will of God for his life. He had run from God's will, fleeing out of a selfish timidity. Moses chose to endure hardship with God's people in Egypt rather than to engage in the "passing pleasures of sin" (Heb. 11:25), but Jonah ran blindly in the opposite direction. Moses looked to the reward from the perspective of godly obedience, but Jonah looked to the "rewards" of selfish indulgence.

22

Empty Behavior?

Just how far *down* will God allow us to go? Those times in which I knew His clear revelation and will for my life, yet turned and went in a different direction, were moments filled with anxiety and frustration. The Lord Jesus described the emptiness of this kind of behavior: "For what will a man be profited, if he gains the whole world, and forfeits his soul? Or what will a man give in exchange for his soul?" (Matt. 16:26). Like crime, disobedience pays no lasting dividends.

You may not be a prophet or prophetess, but God has told you something to do. He has made it clear to your heart through the teaching of the Word of God, the ministry of the Spirit of God, and the circumstances of life designed by God. Is your response still cautious? "Father, this is a little too much to handle. Why not choose someone else? Let my husband do this. Let my wife do this. Let our pastor take this task. Maybe my Sunday School teacher, but not me, Lord!"

Sound familiar? We too easily shove off spiritual responsibility upon recognized "spiritual professionals." The fact that God has made us priests and ministers to Him (Rev. 1:6; 1 Pet. 2:5,9) is cheapened by our self-righteous rationalization in doing God's will. We need to remember the obedience of Christ Himself as He faced the agony of Calvary: "And He went a little beyond them, and fell on His face and prayed, saying 'My Father, if it is possible, let this cup pass from Me; yet not as I will, but as Thou wilt'" (Matt. 26:39).

THE WILL OF GOD MAY NOT
ALWAYS BE WHAT YOU LIKE,
BUT IT IS ALWAYS RIGHT.

Footnotes

1. Robert T. Boyd, *Tells, Tombs and Treasures* (New York: Bonanza Books, 1969), p. 140.
2. Joppa is now known as Jaffa, the well-known port of Israel on the Mediterranean; it was 50 miles from Gath-hepher.

3 | Exposed by the Storm
Jonah 1:4–9

Our week of family activities had finally come to a conclusion. Lynn was now busily engaged in her new role as a happy mother of a wonderful baby boy. Daddy wasn't left out either —we took turns with early morning bottles and dirty diapers! We were delighted with this gift from God, and we wanted to do all the right things that parents do.

Since this was Saturday morning, we looked forward with anticipation to that little extra treat of sleeping in. Lynn's mom had been with us for several weeks since Matthew was born, helping out with sterilizing bottles, washing clothes, cleaning house, and all the countless other responsibilities around our mobile home. But mom was gone now, having flown back to the West Coast.

The coffee pot was busily perking its morning tune when the phone rang. It rang just once before I quickly put the receiver to my ear:

"Good morning!"

"Jimmy—would you please go in and be with Lynn. Daddy died this morning!"

It was one of those moments that you hear about from other people and on TV, but never really think will happen to you! As I raced back to the bedroom my eyes were already cloudy with tears. Lynn could see my face and read a thousand instant thoughts of crisis. She snatched up the extension phone and listened, not really wanting to hear:

"Honey—the Lord has taken our daddy home. He died just a few minutes ago."

We clung to each other in those moments of helplessness. Our tears wet the sheets of our bed and we managed a heart-torn prayer of praise and petition for God's strength and peace. Our minds were exploding with a multitude of thoughts and questions.

Our great storm had come with unexpected fury, but by realizing and resting in God's sovereign grace we weathered this crisis of loss, and it brought us both a step closer to knowing the greatness of our God. For Lynn's mom and the rest of the family the experience was immediately shattering, but in time there was strengthening as God's sovereign grace healed the shock and moved them onward. *God may even use a great storm to bring us to the knowledge of His greatness.*

The Storm on the Sea

With all the circumstances being favorable to Jonah, the prophet must have been relaxing below deck on the ship. He was catching his breath after running away from God's service, from standing before God as His obedient prophet.

But verse 4 brings us back to the Lord's perspective of the situation with the words "and the Lord." Jonah has been on center stage in the opening narrative, but now we encounter the God of all circumstances. His entrance upon the scene is invisible, yet unmistakable. One man has written that God lets men "have their way up to a certain point. He waits, in the tranquility of His Almightiness, until they have completed their preparations; and then, when man has ended, He begins, that man may see the more that it is His doing."[1]

What the Lord did was to literally "throw" or "hurl" a "great wind on the sea." The word suggests the actions of a baseball pitcher who hurls a speeding curveball toward the waiting batter. The action is causative; God is doing it: "And there was a great storm on the sea." Here is both a great storm and a great occasion for a great God!

Now this was no cool breeze off the Columbia River. From the standpoint of the ship itself, the next phrase is picturesque: "So that the ship was about to break up." The literal meaning of this is that "the ship thought itself to be broken

25

up." What a gale! A sturdy vessel, used to the rugged Mediterranean waves pounding against its sides, was now about to come apart at the seams!

Completely unexpected and unmanageable, the storm caused these sailors to react in terror. The text reads in verse 5, "Then the sailors became afraid." A peaceful voyage had been invaded by a persistent God. Previously the sailors had been tending to the routine chores of sailing, but now their response was vastly different—they were terrified! This was unlike any storm they had ever encountered!

The Helpless Gods

"And every man cried to his god" (v. 5). What would you do when pressed to the breaking point in a violent storm? Their response was to turn to their last straw of hope, a polytheistic array of gods! Each man had his own "patron saint." Even today some people put small figurines in their automobiles as their gods of safety in travel.

Polytheism, the worship of many gods, was not some new fad. Jonah had seen this before, even in his own country. The outside influences of foreign nations had turned the hearts of the Israelites toward other gods and religious idols.

The Egyptians were especially noted for their inventory of gods. Everything had a special god: sky, water, houses, fields, cattle, people. In the 10 plagues which the Lord brought upon Egypt (Exod. 7—11), God demonstrated His sovereign power over every god of the Egyptians. His object lesson was clear: There is *no* god but the true God of Israel.

To what or to whom do you go when the storms begin to swell in your life? Is Christ the Lord of your *crises*, or do you just let Him be master over the *comforts*? A crisis experience, a big storm in life, can either *crush* us or *conform* us. We can be crushed by grief, fear, worry, and doubt. Our circumstances can dominate and decimate our peace. They may even control us. On the other hand, we can view any crisis from the perspective of a child: "I don't understand what all this means, but my Father is doing something that He knows is best. I'll leave this matter in His hands." A childlike faith is what the Lord Jesus Christ taught in Matthew 19:14: "But Jesus said, 'Let the children alone, and do not hinder them from coming to Me; for the kingdom of heaven belongs to such as these.' " *Fear* will crush, but *faith* will conform!

A very natural scene was taking place aboard the ship. Men were frightened and crying out to their personal gods. Panic was beginning to grip their hearts. "And they threw the cargo which was in the ship into the sea to lighten it for them." Were these grown men having a temper tantrum? Hardly. The storm was reaching a peak of great intensity, and these old salts knew that to lighten the vessel of extra weight would allow them to ride the waves more easily. So their books, bottles, trunks, chairs, and even their cargo were hurled into the sea. In this way they hoped to improve their chances for survival. The sailors probably felt like the storm was riding on their backs!

The Sleeping Prophet

You would think that with all the commotion on deck—the captain shouting orders to his crew, screaming passengers being tossed to and fro with each jolting wave—that no one could escape the panic. "But Jonah had gone below into the hold of the ship, lain down, and fallen asleep." Imagine that! Asleep! Jonah had gone down into the innermost part of the ship, into the "thigh" of the vessel, and had found a place to lie down. This was now his private stateroom. He had tucked himself away from the danger and confusion of the stormy crisis.

Jonah had fallen into a deep sleep. How some people can manage to fall asleep with a clanging cacophony of noise nearby is an unknown art. How could he do this? What was his secret? Did he take a few Sominex sleeping pills along in his prophet's pouch? Several answers have been proposed. Perhaps Jonah was just exhausted after his lengthy flight. Maybe he hoped to escape the storm and wake up to a calm sea. Did he think he had reached safety away from God? Could it be that his slumber was in his false security of selfishness? Or did he, with a conscience filled with the throbbing realization of sin, try to sleep his conscience clear? We can't know definitely, but more than likely Jonah's ability to fall into such a tranquil state of repose was due to a combination of these factors.

Have you ever been mesmerized by the mystery of sleep? Have you ever tried to sleep sin away? I have. I remember times when I went to bed early, foolishly thinking that when I woke up all would be well. What I wanted to avoid through sleep was only compounded from the delay of allowing God to deal with it. The lesson of the book of Jonah is that if we fall asleep to the corrective voice of God, He may have to awaken us suddenly with a traumatic event!

Jonah was learning that *our great God may even use a great storm to bring us to the knowledge of His greatness.*

The Search on the Ship

Before long the intensity of the search for the cause of the storm became almost as violent as the storm itself. Desperation swept through the decks! The whole ship was buzzing with theories, and the sailors turned to their gods in fear.

What a different setting for the Christian! The apostle John writes in his letter that "there is no fear in love; but perfect love casts out fear, because fear involves punishment, and the one who fears is not perfected in love" (1 John 4:18). We can have confidence in a Lord who does not love on the basis of our human performance, but initiates His transforming work in our hearts through the effective expression of His gracious, unconditional love (1 John 4:19). Fear is out of the question in this kind of climate! No phobias here! Instead of an old man with a big stick, we find a loving Father who encourages us to faithful obedience.

God often chooses to reveal Himself through great crises. In times like these, He often allows us to search until we come to the end of ourselves!

The sailors' emergency situation called for some authority, so the next character in the drama now enters the scene. "So the captain approached him [Jonah] and said, 'How is it that you are sleeping?' " (v. 6). The implication of the captain's question was, "How could you be sleeping at a time like this?" We are not told why the ship's master was down in the lower deck. Perhaps he came down to check on the safety of the passengers or to enlist more help to fight the raging storm. His next words to Jonah rose him from his sleep: "Get up, call on your god!"

Poor Jonah! He couldn't even manage a restful nap before being awakened with the very same words that he had heard the Lord say to him in verse 2: "Arise!" I wonder what Jonah's immediate impression was upon hearing the captain's voice. Surely the captain had to speak several times in order to disturb such a deep sleep. Did Jonah think he was dreaming? Did he feel for one fleeting moment that God was speaking to him again, that God had found his secret hiding place?

The rest of the command dispelled any such notion. "Call on your god!" The definite article is used in the phrase, and it can therefore be translated "Call, cry out, to *the* God of yours." The captain certainly wanted everyone to appeal to his personal god, and perhaps this Jewish stranger had a god, the true God, who could help them. "Perhaps your God will be concerned about us, so we won't die."

Do we call on God in a last-ditch effort to pull us through some stormy mess we're in? Is ours a last-minute faith? The shipmaster was beginning to see that a new Master was needed here.

Casting Lots

Now that all the excess baggage and cargo were floating in the deep, the sailors tried another angle. "And each man said to his mate, 'Come, let us cast lots, so we may learn on whose account this calamity has struck us' " (v. 7).

These men were resorting to a common practice involving lots. We would probably call this "drawing straws." The drawing of lots was used in deciding matters, in dividing articles or property, and for consulting purposes. Proverbs 18:18 tells us, "The lot puts an end to contentions, and decides between the mighty." In the decision to replace Judas in the company of the 12 apostles, the lot was drawn, and Matthias was chosen and numbered with the 11 apostles (Acts 1:23-26). Zacharias, the father of John the Baptist, was selected by lot to enter the Temple of the Lord to burn incense (Luke 1:9). This procedure was not viewed as any chance operation for Proverbs 16:33 states, "The lot is cast into the lap, but its every decision is from the Lord." God is sovereign even in the business of drawing straws.

"The lot fell on Jonah." By the sovereign design of God the lot discovered the culprit, for it was Jonah who got the short straw. So now the investigation intensified as the mariners began to throw a battery of questions at Jonah. They wanted to get to the bottom of this mystery right away, even if it took a kangaroo court to accomplish the task!

The Inquisitors

The sailors said to him, "Tell us now" (v. 8). These men were not in any mood to beat around the bush. They demanded answers *now!* "On whose account has this calamity struck us? What is your occupation? And where do you come from? What is your country? From what people are you?" This courtroom scene aboard the ship began to assume the character of a prosecuting attorney striking for convicting information!

These questions must have sliced into the privacy of Jonah's conscience like a sharpened razor blade! "What is your occupation?"

"A prophet of God"—the office of privilege and honor from which Jonah had fled!

"And where do you come from?"

"From Israel—from standing obediently and humbly before my God."

"What is your country? From what people are you?"

"The people of God, those divinely chosen by Him to be His very own possession." Jonah had deserted them and joined himself to this unbelieving company of pagan sailors. Instead of being a light to them with the truth of God, he was asking them to serve his selfish purposes. Jonah's fear was smothering the light of his witness.

As Jonah pondered these questions within his own heart, the truth must have been painfully revealing. He was beginning to see himself in the light of God's truth. And His truth is designed to cut through such conditions (Heb. 4:12). It has penetrating power! Sometimes spiritual surgery is required to alleviate suffering due to sin. The prosecuting attorneys in this case were beginning to lay bare the facts. The discovery of sin is not a pretty operation, but it is absolutely necessary for life. Spiritual diagnosis by God's light is mandatory. Sometimes the divine Surgeon must *cut* before he can *cure*. So it was with Jonah. He had to learn that *the Lord may use a great storm to bring us to the knowledge of His greatness.*

Jonah was finding that this process is painful. Hebrews 12:11 reminds us that "all discipline for the moment seems not to be joyful, but sorrowful; yet to those who have been trained by it, afterwards it yields the peaceful fruit of righteousness."

Confession of a Rebel

Jonah begins by answering the last question first, since the first inquiries had hit too close to his heart. "And he said to them, 'I am a Hebrew'" (v. 9). He selects a word that was commonly used to distinguish the people of God from those of other nations. The distinctiveness of his people must have left an impression on Jonah's mind.

Without further comment, Jonah continues, "And I fear the Lord God of heaven, who made the sea and the dry land"! His admission of fear was not that of fright. Jonah confessed his deep, reverential trust in Yahweh, his God. As he opened his mouth and the words of faith tumbled from his lips, the ministry of the Spirit of God must have swept over him. This phrase did not focus on any of the questions put to him, but rather drove him to realize the very character of God. Creator! Sovereign Lord! The land and even this tumultuous sea were in subjection to Him! "Yes, I am a Hebrew. My God is Yahweh! He is the Almighty Creator!"

Can you feel the sacred reality of this moment? The prophet's heart must have burned within him. "How could I

31

have run from this God?" The greatness of God filled Jonah's entire being.

Did you note how Jonah referred to his God before these sailors? "Lord God," a compound title of majesty and praise. This statement from the heart contains important lessons for us. One such lesson concerns the way we address our Lord. How do we use His name? Into which context do we place Him? Do we refer to Him as "Jesus" in some flippant, dishonoring manner, as do certain bumper stickers? How often do we proclaim His full name, the Lord Jesus Christ?

Perhaps you have trouble with His name because you are unsure of His true character—who He really is. Do you equate the Lord Jesus Christ with "putting a tiger in your tank," or is He the sovereign Lord of your life, the very God-man, the glorified Christ of God, the triumphant King?

Jonah's heart of selfishness was being crushed by a great God who loved him; His Sovereign Majesty left this runaway prophet with little else to say. The prosecution was about to close its case; God was about to show Jonah His power.

> OUR GREAT GOD MAY EVEN USE
> A GREAT STORM TO BRING US TO
> THE KNOWLEDGE OF HIS GREATNESS.

Footnote

1. E. B. Pusey, "Jonah," *Barnes on the Old Testament, The Minor Prophets*, vol. 1 (Grand Rapids: Baker Book House, 1973).

4 | When All Else Fails
Jonah 1:10–12

What do you do when you have really blown it? How do you make up for wrongs done? When you've disciplined one of your children in red-hot anger, or when you've hurt your wife or husband with a cutting comment, or when you've impatiently done some automobile acrobatics on the freeway, what do you do about it?

Some of us hide, others try to forget, and a few of us choose to completely forget the whole situation. But what is the correct response? To deal honestly and sensitively with the problem at hand. But how can we do this? What is our responsibility when sin has gained its mastery over us at any given moment? For Jonah, the mariners' bombarding questions were being used by God to bring the weight of conviction upon the disobedient prophet.

As we draw open the curtain on verses 10-12, the renegade Jonah is still in the witness chair. His questioners are bearing down on him, and the questions are striking close to home! This dramatic scene is taking place right in the middle of the Mediterranean Sea. The Judge of all the earth is revealing His righteous indignation as the seas become increasingly stormy. The waves are tempestuous, and so are Jonah's inner feelings! Yet God's peace does not come through rebellion, but through a restful surrender. This is exactly what Jonah needed to learn. *Only a surrendered life will experience the peace of God.*

The Sailors' Questions

Verse 10 asks literally, "What is this that you have done?"

Poor Jonah! This accusation must have penetrated like a stake driven into the ground. Imagine yourself being in Jonah's situation. "What's the problem with you?" Oh, that hurts! And from a group of unbelieving sailors at that!

Sometimes it takes a question like this to really open our eyes to our own unbelief. I wonder what went through the minds of those men as they confronted Jonah with their final blow. Had his God treated him unfairly? Had he tired of God? Did he find that God was unworthy? Jonah was crushed by the knockout punch!

But after Jonah's acknowledgement of his disobedience to the great God of Israel and the universe, it was the sailors' turn to become knocked down.

The literal text of verse 10 says, "They feared a great fear." Why? Not because the boat was getting swamped with water, but because of the reality of God's presence. Jonah had told the crew all about his flight from God's presence, and now they had put the puzzle together correctly and realized that something supernatural was at hand. The men were afraid of the power and righteousness of God.

A tremendous amount of divine activity is coming into focus here, both in Jonah and in the sailors themselves. God was not only moving the waters, but He was also moving the hearts! It is this quality of fear that will lead to a converted heart.

What Is the Solution?

Now that the sailors knew the *why* of their predicament, the next task was to discover the *what* of the solution. So the men confront Jonah with their dilemma: "What should we do to you that the sea may become calm for us?" The verb used in verse 11 means "to be quiet or silent" (see also Ps. 107:30 and Prov. 26:20). How they all longed for the calmness they once had known!

In their confrontation the crew showed a certain respect toward the disobedient prophet by asking him the solution to their problem. Note the irony of the scene: They might have been surmising, "So Jonah didn't want to share Yahweh's word of mercy with the Ninevites, but will he now speak to save us?" Their question put the responsibility squarely upon Jonah's shoulder! What he had been running from he now must face.

God had brought Jonah to a fork in the road; it was clearly an either/or situation. The sailors leaned forward, anxiously awaiting his decision.

Have you ever been forced into the position of having to answer a similar question: "What are you going to do about this?" This is no time for weak-kneed believers! Action is demanded—we must stop our praying and begin doing. This is exactly the admonition that James gives: "But prove yourselves doers of the word, and not merely hearers who delude themselves" (Jas. 1:22).

We need not travel too far from home in order to gain an eyeful of how human nature operates. One Friday evening I had planned to stop at a nearby TV repair shop on my way home from church. As I drove up to the front of the store I found myself right in the middle of a vicious argument. Four irate women stood with flashing tongues on one side, while a defensive shop proprietor stood on the other.

The gist of the fireworks was that the owner had ordered a car towed away that belonged to one of the ladies. She had violated his parking space in order to visit an adjacent store. Nervously I walked right through the middle of this no man's land and placed my television set on the counter. As I returned, the combatants were still deeply engaged in battle. Cautiously I stepped in and said, "Who is *really* at fault here?"

"Well, I don't know," the women's spokesperson blurted out, "but we parked our car here for only 10 or 15 minutes. When we came out our car was gone!"

"I see. What are you going to do now?" This question seemed to hang in the air for a few seconds.

The women, almost red with disgust, looked speechlessly at one another. The question had landed a quieting blow as they realized that the blame rested with their side. A few eyes were swollen to the point of tears as the ladies thundered off in a rage. It's amazing what happens when we are asked to do something, to put our hands to the task!

This situation was similar to that which Jonah faced. What was he going to do about his situation now? Avoid it, hide from it, ignore it, or face it according to God's design? He needed to learn that *only a surrendered life will experience the peace of God.*

The two convicting questions had found their mark. Verse 12 is rich: "And he said to them, 'Pick me up and throw me into the sea. Then the sea will become calm for you, for I know that on account of me this great storm has come upon you.' "

Notice the four elements in this verse: Jonah's sin, surrender, sacrifice, and satisfaction.

Jonah's Sin

The prophet's rebellion brought remorse to God. Jonah recognized his sin: "I know that on account of me—" These are tough words in any vocabulary! In one sense it is perhaps the most difficult phrase that one could utter. There is no chance in the world for people like you and me to admit fault in such a drastic situation unless the Lord is moving our hearts.

Jonah said, "I know—" The same word is used in verse 10 in reference to the sailors: "For the men *knew* that he fled from the presence of the Lord" (italics added). This is a discriminatory, discerning, personal type of knowing. Jonah had time to consider his life, and now he really *knew* he was a sinner; he really knew he had blown it before God! Jonah recognized his wrong, his selfishness, his disobedience, and his fear of men.

Not only did he properly evaluate the immediate predicament, but he was also becoming aware of the fact that continued sin affects others. Like a spreading, cancerous growth, Jonah's sinful flight from God had pulled these mariners into the same boiling pot to suffer the same consequences.

No one "drowns" alone. Paul talks about this in 2 Corinthians 2:5. He says in effect, "Friend, if you think you're causing me some problems, forget it! You're giving the *whole church* something that is causing sorrow!" The living members of Christ's church are to be so intimately related in fellowship that "if one member suffers, all the members suffer with it" (1 Cor. 12:26). God's Spirit has placed all of us into one body, the Church (see 1 Cor. 12:13). That's why we hurt when others hurt. That's why it is such a privilege to rejoice when another family member is honored (see 1 Cor. 12:26).

Perhaps you are in Jonah's position right now: As a Christian you are suffering under the crushing weight of your own sin, and the storm of God's conviction is drawing its verdict. Others are suffering too—perhaps your family or your local assembly or the people with whom you work. What should you do? First *confess*, then *surrender*. Jonah sets the pace.

Jonah's Surrender

The weakling became strong as Jonah's repentance met God's request. The prophet finally gave in; he came to the point where he said, "Lord, I see it now; I see myself in your light. I'm through trying to hold back; I'm tired of rationalizing my actions!" Jonah's surrender is seen in the form of repentance: He became ready to change his mind about his own life and the direction he had been pursuing.

We can't surrender until we see our own sin, and that usually comes at the point of defeat. Picture in your mind a military general in his magnificent uniform with troops assembled to his right and tactical weapons positioned to his left. Imagine how ridiculous it would be for him to hold up his little finger at this point and say, "I give up!" We wouldn't know how to handle a situation like this.

But what do you and I do? Instead of giving the Lord complete control of our lives by the empowering of the Holy Spirit (see Eph. 5:18), we wait until our sin is ready to crush us! Then, at the point of final despair we seek out a few grunts, "Okay, Lord, take it!" Haven't we learned anything from Jacob in Genesis 32? God had to physically wrestle with the "supplanter" and pin him to the mat in order to get through!

My father-in-law had a quick wit. He used to say repeated-

37

ly, "Jim, God will let you be as miserable as you want to be!" This is exactly where Jonah was living. The sovereign will of God had allowed him to run to the place where he was sick of his own life and of its effect upon these innocent bystanders. Instead of receiving God's peace, he got a storm!

Why do we insist on playing games with our all-knowing Father? Do you have a certain habit in your life that is plaguing you? You've tried to break it, but it has continued to run you down and defeat you. Maybe it's secret; maybe only a few others know. But it's still there! Have you come to that point of honesty before God and admitted to Him that the reason you're still under bondage is because deep within you enjoy that sin?

We reserve a special pocket within the character of our lives for that particular habit, and we're reluctant to let God reach in and take it away! Perhaps we fear the loss of pleasure or status. Whatever the reason, we need to ask God to clean out those secret pockets!

David captures these very thoughts as a personal challenge in Psalm 51:6,7,10: "Behold, Thou dost desire truth in the innermost being, and in the hidden part Thou wilt make me know wisdom. Purify me with hyssop, and I shall be clean; wash me, and I shall be whiter than snow. . . . Create in me a clean heart, O God, and renew a steadfast spirit within me."

Once again David echoes our need. He puts the pickax to work in the inward chambers of the heart when he cries, "Search me, O God, and know my heart; try me and know my anxious thoughts; and see if there be any hurtful way in me, and lead me in the everlasting way" (Ps. 139:23,24).

Do you know why the storm is still raging, and in fact getting rougher and rougher? Because sin is still in the ship. Jonah is on deck! *Only a surrendered life will experience the peace of God.*

What do you do with a young believer who comes to this point in his life? What you *don't* say is, "It's tremendous to see that you've received Jesus Christ. I'm so happy for you! Isn't God wonderful in His work of grace and providence! Now the first thing you must do is this: Cut out all your bad

38

habits. Once you get them out of your life, and clean up your dress and behavior, you can join us at church!" Does this sound farfetched? Believers often convey this very attitude, even if these exact words are not spoken. We expect a new believer to just wipe his slate clean, purging all the ugliness out of his life instantaneously and walking immediately as a mature person in Christ.

Jonah was not a novice. He had been God's prophet for some years. The point is that in the lives of both young or old, God will do the changing according to His own gracious timetable. As Ecclesiastes 3:1 reveals, "There is an appointed time for everything. And there is a time for every event under heaven." Now was Jonah's time!

Jonah's Sacrifice

Three words crack through the deafening silence: "Pick me up." Literally, "You take me, you lift me up." Why didn't Jonah just jump overboard? That would have been so easy, so neat in execution. "Hey, Jonah, why don't you just climb up on the rail and hop off?"

If these were the unspoken thoughts of the sailors, they certainly did not understand this prophet very well. Jonah knew that he was in the hands of a sovereign God, the Giver of life and Author of all creation. For him to have jumped into the engulfing waves would be a sin in itself. He would be taking his own life. Jonah had no right or authority to do that!

In 2 Samuel 24:17 we have the historical context in which King David numbered the people. He was being influenced by Satan (see 1 Chron. 21:1). Notice what David says here, and then relate this incident to the situation facing Jonah: "Then David spoke to the Lord when he saw the angel who was striking down the people, and said, 'Behold, it is I who have sinned, and it is I who have done wrong; but these sheep, what have they done? Please let Thy hand be against me and against my father's house.' "

David was ready to be a willing sacrifice for his own people. Jonah stood in the same position, though his audience was hardly Jewish! There he was: He did not want to go to Nineveh, and he was reluctant to preach God's message of mercy and repentance to his enemies.

The beginning brush strokes of a portrait of the Lord Jesus Christ are being painted here. Christ the Lord came into human history as God made flesh. But there are several great differences even in the context of similarity. Jesus was the perfect man, without sin (Heb. 4:15). Jonah realized his sin and surrendered himself. Jesus realized *my* sin, yet He surrendered Himself for me! "But God demonstrates His own love toward us, in that while we were yet sinners, Christ died for us" (Rom. 5:8).

The Lord Jesus stood in our place. In writing to the believers at Ephesus, Paul exhorts them to be "mimics" of God who are walking in love, "just as Christ also loved you, and gave Himself up for us, an offering and a sacrifice to God as a fragrant aroma" (Eph. 5:1,2). What a vein of gold is packed into such short words! The three-letter word "for" in "gave Himself up *for* us" means literally "instead of" or "in behalf of." This is an expression of sacrificial substitution: Jesus took our place as a willing sacrifice! He was the Lamb of God (see John 1:29). This theme of sacrifice is beautifully depicted in the book of Hebrews:

"But when Christ appeared as a high priest of the good things to come, He entered through the greater and more perfect tabernacle, not made with hands, that is to say, not of this creation; and not through the blood of goats and calves, but through His own blood, He entered the holy place once for all, having obtained eternal redemption. . . . Nor was it that He should offer Himself often, as the high priest enters the holy place year by year with blood not his own . . . . And every priest stands daily ministering and offering time after time the same sacrifices, which can never take away sins; but He, having offered one sacrifice for sins for all time, sat down at the right hand of God" (Heb. 9:11,12,25; 10:11,12).

Jonah is a "type" of Christ. This biblical term is quite simple; it simply means a picture of something else, a small snapshot of a larger portrait. One author has defined a type as "an Old Testament illustration which, while having a place and purpose in biblical history, also is divinely appointed to foreshadow some New Testament truth."

Jonah had reached a decision; he had become a picture of willing sacrifice to die in the place of others. Unlike Jonah, our Lord did not die for His own sin, for He had none. Jonah's resolution would meet God's requirements.

Jonah's Satisfaction

"Then the sea will become calm for you" (v. 12). Jonah spelled out the results for the crew. Not only would the turmoil and tumult of the waves become silent, but the very hand of God's disciplining wrath would also subside. Peace without and peace within! God would soon do His work.

Another prophet, Isaiah, writes a poignant word about this: "But the Lord was pleased to crush Him, putting Him to grief; if He would render Himself as a guilt offering, He will see His offspring, He will prolong His days, and the good pleasure of the Lord will prosper in his hand. As a result of the anguish of His soul, He will see it and be satisfied; by His knowledge the Righteous One, My Servant, will justify the many, as He will bear their iniquities" (Isa. 53:10,11).

There is divine satisfaction in the heart of God when we come to the point of willing surrender. God had to "crush" His Servant, the Lord Jesus Christ. The sovereign control of our glorious Lord was manifested at Calvary: "This Man, delivered up by the predetermined plan and foreknowledge of God, you nailed to a cross by the hands of godless men and put Him to death" (Acts 2:23).

The cross was no mistake! God was not "asleep at the switch" when the trials were held and the verdict rendered and the spikes driven into Jesus' flesh! The very heart of God's program is loving sacrifice.

Jonah anticipated a positive response to God's work— peace. He counted on the fact that God *will* work! God can do the same for us today.

ONLY A SURRENDERED LIFE
WILL EXPERIENCE THE PEACE OF GOD.

5 | If at First You Don't Succeed
Jonah 1:13,14

The drama on board the battered vessel has now reached its climax. Jonah is ready to taste a bit of the brine! But now something intervenes. Verse 13 relates: "However, the men rowed desperately to return to land, but they could not, for the sea was becoming even stormier against them."

Jonah hadn't expected this! He was all prepared for a dive off the port bow! Hadn't he confessed? Hadn't he told the crew what he wanted them to do? Everything seemed wrapped in a nice, neat package, so why the delay in sending Jonah to the bottom?

Let's review what took place in verse 12, noticing those three little words again, "Pick me up." Jonah is not about to disobey his God again at this point! He will not jump. So who does that leave us with? The tired travelers of the sea, the crew themselves! The responsibility has shifted 180 degrees, and now the weight of decision is on the mariners!

What should they do? What is the responsible thing to do in carrying out the will of God at this point? What would *you* do?

If you were a sailor, your immediate response would probably have been just like theirs. The men turned to the area of their specialty. They grabbed their oars and dug into the waves! The oars plunged deep into the water as they sought to conquer the stubborn storm.

Man Against God

The old salts gave it all they had. They were determined!

42

Just like us, they were grasping for the brass ring, for something to satisfy Jonah's God and find peace. We too dig into this good program or that meaningful life-style. Sometimes we find that our futile efforts are frustrated—like trying to dig through a brick wall with our bare fingernails!

Row hard, men! Maybe just one more stroke or one more good work added to our list.... Maybe if we just tact on enough admirable things God will grant us the peace we seek! But now these Phoenician sailors were about to learn a crucially important lesson from Jonah's great God: *Apart from faithful obedience, man's efforts cannot satisfy God's requirements.*

It must have been quite a sight as Jonah watched the mariners put their sinewy hands and muscles to the task. Their talents were pitched against a powerful competitor—God Himself! "But they could not, for the sea was becoming even stormier against them." How picturesque is the literal language at this juncture! The sea was "walking, moving, and raging upon them." You've heard the slang expression, "they walked all over us!" Perhaps you've used that phrase in sports competition to describe the devastating defeat of one team by another. That's the sense of the Hebrew here. The waves, moved along by the invisible hand of Yahweh, were walking all over the boat, the sailors, the disobedient prophet, and their entire display of self-effort! God was literally putting a wet blanket on their short-sighted strivings. Good works are not good when faithful obedience is a missing ingredient!

The Prayer of Desperation

Though the men were trying their best as their oars churned up the water, they realized it was a lost cause. Now what? "Well, if we can't get God's appeasement through determined practice, then maybe we can shoot up a few desperate prayers! Perhaps a little religion will be just the ticket! We've tried everything else, so why not give it a whirl?"

"Then they *called* on the Lord" (v. 14). This particular word is used eight times in the narrative (see 1:2,6,14; 2:2; 3:2,4,5,8) and is elsewhere translated "proclaim," "cry," "invite," and "name." In ancient times the term was used to signify the reading aloud of the Old Testament Scriptures. The New Testament parallel to this word is "preach."

The old salts were trembling in their boots. This desperate cry was their ace in the hole, their trump card. But notice that they called out to God—to *Jonah's* God, Yahweh! It was an intense effort. Echoes of an earlier era come to mind as we recall the phrase in Genesis 4:26, "Then men began to call upon the name of the Lord." Was God finally getting through?

Only moments before in this traumatic experience each man had called out to his personal god to come to the rescue. But God had been working on these sailors' hearts, and the evidence of this fact was now being verbally sounded out!

Why Do We Pray?

A few years ago my son Matthew developed a very cagey technique. When he knew that the discipline stick was about to make an impression on his "blessed assurance," he would reverently lower his little head. Then, in a flawless maneuver, he would quickly drop to his knees, fold his hands together and say, "Daddy, let's pray!" During this "performance" Lynn and I could hardly keep a straight face! Here was desperate prayer before discipline! Matt attempted his best to divert the disaster, but still the discipline was applied.

As I survey my own life I can vividly recall the Lord's working in my own heart. During my junior year at college I was living in a boardinghouse. The policy there was that any student could help reduce his board and payments by doing some of the chores around the home. Interestingly enough, the name of that place was *Allerlie*, a German word meaning "all sorts of things." An appropriate title indeed! For that is exactly what characterized the life-style of its occupants.

Some of those early-morning college parties on the weekends found me flopping into bed at 4 A.M. Do you know what I started to do? I began praying. God was at work in the quiet chambers of my heart, troubling me and probing my conscience.

What was going on? No one was preaching to me, and no one had explained how I could know the Saviour in a personal way. But I found myself uttering something to God. Sometimes those prayers were ritualistic—a desperate attempt to find a quick antidote for my convicted mind. But at other times I felt that I was really connecting with Someone! And still God kept after me, evoking the desire to call out to Him. He was etching His presence upon my being.

Don't Let Us Die

Let's note the desperate prayer of these men: "We earnestly pray, O Lord, do not let us perish on account of this man's life and do not put innocent blood on us; for Thou, O Lord, hast done as Thou hast pleased." As we examine these words we find several interesting features. *First, these men employed a very strong expression of entreating here.* It's not, "Lord, are you up there?" but rather, "We earnestly pray, O Yahweh!" Sincerity is beginning to saturate their motives.

The second observation to be made is the honest confession of the seeking sailors: "O Lord, do not let us perish on account of this man's life and do not put innocent blood on us." What they were really saying was that just in case they had made a mistake about this matter with Jonah by tossing an innocent man over the side, "Please Lord, don't zap us dead!"

Perhaps they had heard of the teaching of the Torah from Jewish contacts in their business ventures. The shedding of a man's blood was a phrase used to represent the taking of his life, for "the life of all flesh [is] its blood" (Lev. 17:14; see also Jon. 1:14; Prov. 28:17; Ezek. 33:6).

How conscious they were of the possibility of destroying an innocent life! Godly fear is in evidence here. "We don't want his blood on our consciences!" Compare this to Paul's statement in Acts 20:26.

Hasty recruitment can spell disaster if not done according to the will of God. Paul warns Timothy in this regard: "Do not lay hands upon any one too hastily and thus share responsibility for the sins of others; keep yourself free from sin" (1 Tim. 5:22).

A Life-or-Death Matter

I want you to take note of an interesting principle here. The tip-off is found in the small word "put" in the phrase "do not put innocent blood on us." The King James Version translates this word as "lay." Jonah has already used this word in verse 3, when he bought a ticket for the trip to Tarshish. The word for "pay" is the same term as "put" or "lay" in verse 14.

When Jonah offered to pay the ship's fare, there was no hesitation by the sailors in accepting the coins. But now that he has asked these same men to pick him up and give him the heave-ho, their response is wholly different!

Money is one thing, but a man's life is quite another matter. On the one hand they accepted his money, but on the other hand they weren't about to be responsible for his life.

Can you think of a similar set of circumstances in the New Testament? There was a man who accepted money in the time of Jesus. As Jonah betrayed God, so there was Judas who betrayed the Son of God—and received his secret payment in silver coins.

Matthew 27:24 records the well-known incident of still another man who, in front of a multitude of onlookers, washed his hands. The symbolic significance of this act was powerful! Pontius Pilate, the governor, refused to assume any responsibility for the life of Jesus; he wanted to wash his hands of the whole affair. His statement was similar to that uttered by these sailors: "I am innocent of this Man's blood; see to that yourselves."

Why point out these similarities? Only to show that this situation in the middle of the sea was being used by God to cut through the sailors' outward facade. This was not some minor issue of commerce or exchange, but the issue of life itself! Jonah's life and their own lives were hanging in the balance. Through His sovereign maneuvering of time and circumstances, God had brought these mariners to the place where they stood face-to-face with the Author of life!

The Sovereignty of God

The third element of this prayer is that God's sovereignty was recognized and exalted: "Thou, O Lord, hast done as Thou hast pleased." This is the psalmist's theme of praise as he says, "Whatever the Lord pleases, He does, in heaven and in earth, in the seas and in all deeps .... But our God is in the heavens; He does whatever He pleases" (Ps. 135:6; 115: 3).

One of the New Testament verses that continues this thread of truth is found in Philippians 2:13: "For it is God who is at work in you, both to will and to work for His good pleasure."

It is so gloriously evident that the Spirit of God is in control here! These unbelieving seafarers have finally arrived at the same point as had Jonah—surrender to the will of God. The crisis of the moment has transported them to the very crux of life—our relationship to our Creator.

The pounding of the waves and the positive witness of the fleeing prophet had made clear God's presence. Heaven waited for their response. Would they, *could* they find the peace of God? The triumphant stanza of John Newton's hymn, "Amazing Grace," could have been whistling through the salty air:

> Through many dangers, toils, and snares
> I have already come;
> 'Tis grace hath brought me safe thus far,
> And grace will lead me home.

Our God is a specialist in breaking the hardened heart. This moment was no exception!

Before moving on to the final three exciting verses in chapter 1, let's take a quick inventory and see just how applicable Jonah's responses are to our own lives! What *should* we do when we sin? (See page 48.)

Our tendency is to "do our own thing." Like the sailors, and like Jonah, we impulsively dart off to try to accomplish some good works for God. Let's be reminded of our theme in this chapter:

APART FROM FAITHFUL OBEDIENCE,
MAN'S EFFORTS CANNOT SATISFY GOD'S REQUIREMENTS.

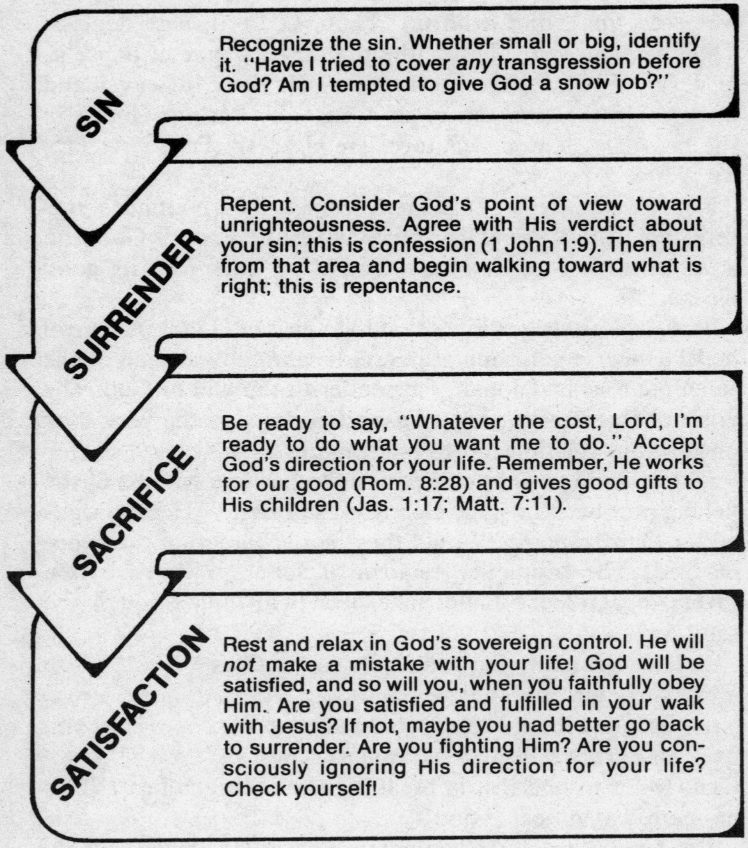

SIN

Recognize the sin. Whether small or big, identify it. "Have I tried to cover *any* transgression before God? Am I tempted to give God a snow job?"

SURRENDER

Repent. Consider God's point of view toward unrighteousness. Agree with His verdict about your sin; this is confession (1 John 1:9). Then turn from that area and begin walking toward what is right; this is repentance.

SACRIFICE

Be ready to say, "Whatever the cost, Lord, I'm ready to do what you want me to do." Accept God's direction for your life. Remember, He works for our good (Rom. 8:28) and gives good gifts to His children (Jas. 1:17; Matt. 7:11).

SATISFACTION

Rest and relax in God's sovereign control. He will *not* make a mistake with your life! God will be satisfied, and so will you, when you faithfully obey Him. Are you satisfied and fulfilled in your walk with Jesus? If not, maybe you had better go back to surrender. Are you fighting Him? Are you consciously ignoring His direction for your life? Check yourself!

Diagram 2

6 | He Ate the Whole Thing!
Jonah 1:15–17

Home canning! Widemouth jars, sealing lids, sticky syrups, and fussy mixes—the whole kitchen becomes a production line. Cherries, peaches, apricots, applesauce, and maybe a few vegetables—anything you can put into a glass container gets canned! Perhaps you have an industrious and thrifty mother who has gone through the canning process, or maybe this is a yearly ritual around your own home. Homecanning is quite an ordeal and involves some hard work, but it sure does provide some good eating later on!

Have you noticed one simple fact about canning? Before you are able to *preserve*, you must *possess* the product. Those blackberries that come from the thorny bushes had to be *secured* before they could be *preserved*. The home canning process is very much like the spiritual process: *God will faithfully preserve that which He fully possesses.*

As we come to the end of chapter 1 of Jonah, God is in the "canning business"! He is in the process of taking a disobedient prophet and sovereignly "preserving" him. But instead of using a glass jar, the Lord uses a great fish.

Over the Side!

A stranger had boarded a Phoenician vessel sailing for Tarshish, but a strange storm violently interrupted the journey, and so a mad dash was made to find the cause of this blustery gale. The ship quickly became the platform for an intense interrogation, and soon the series of questions struck home— Jonah was the culprit!

The discovery, the confession, and the surrender have all led up to this final moment. Alternative efforts have proved useless, and now the moment of decision is upon the sailors; effective action is the only choice remaining!

In verse 15 we read a very simple and concise statement: "So they picked up Jonah, threw him into the sea, and the sea stopped its raging." How brief, yet to the point! They *really did it*—man overboard!

Those old salts literally lifted Jonah off his feet and tossed him over the side! And suddenly the rushing waves became like glass as nature was hushed.

How do you picture this incident? I can remember various incidents from my army basic training. "Home" was a rather drab-looking barracks in which 50 to 60 men shared their living quarters. All of us were comrades in adjusting to a life-style quite unlike that which we had known earlier.

Any military trainee soon learns to respect the commanding presence of an officer. When he barks an order you had better snap to it! Whenever an officer stepped into our barracks, the first man to spot him in the doorway would holler out "Attention!" All around the barracks there would be a frantic shuffling of feet and rustling of men—then an immediate, whisperless silence as each recruit stopped in his tracks and stood stiffly to attention. That command of "Attention!" turned our circus of activity into a morgue of silence!

When Jonah hit the water it was as if God shouted "Attention!" to the violent gale; the Commander-in-Chief had spoken! I wonder if the response of these stunned sailors was similar to that of the disciples in Mark 6:51: "And they were greatly astonished." We might say that the power and authority of God really "blew their minds!"

God and the Heathen

Jonah 1:15 contains four points worthy of our attention. *First, notice that even the unbelieving mariners could be significantly used by God in carrying out His will.*

Have you ever had that happen in your life? Perhaps you have encountered someone who showed no personal desire to know who Jesus is or why He came. Maybe it was a person who argued with you about your stand for Christ, who kept needling away to see if he could trip you or force you into some theological trap.

Perhaps during the conversation this antagonistic person made a critical observation about your personal life and your Christian testimony. Those words cut deeply; they hurt! But the more you pondered his statement, the more God seemed to be using it to reveal some rust in your armor (see Eph. 6:11-17). This unbelieving critic may very well have been God's "sandpaper" in rubbing off a few jagged edges of carnality in your character!

The second point to notice is that Jonah did not struggle or refuse the direction of God's will.

Now read again what these men did: "They picked up Jonah." Notice that the text does *not* describe how these rugged men chased Jonah all over the deck so they could grab him. They did not play a game of hide-and-seek! There was no struggle here! Pusey quotes Jerome as saying that the sailors "but *lifted* him; as it were, bearing him with respect and honor, they cast him into the sea, not resisting, but yielding himself to their will."[1]

Submitting to God's Will

I think of my own life, when God has clearly directed my steps to do a certain activity or to talk with a certain person. Sometimes there emerged not a resigned willingness but some of those internal murmurings: "Oh, Lord, why did you give me this part-time job? What am I contributing here? I want to serve you in a prominent ministry, not in some little place that is barely on the map!" Or this: "My husband gets to go out to lunch at the office and has a good time with *his* friends, but here *I* am stuck at home!" These small, intrapersonal conversations of discontent are a reflection of an unwilling internal attitude. Perhaps we should just come right out and say, "Lord, I don't like what you're doing with my life. I can't trust your sovereign control!" This is what God hears!

But Jonah is not saying such things. His murmurings are

51

over. He has arrived at the place where he can say, "Father, I'm *willing* to accept whatever you decide to do with me." No longer does he choose to argue with God.

Have we come to that place? Perhaps we need to review Paul's secret of contentment, his single-minded purpose that affected his entire life, "that I may know Him" (Phil. 3:10). Paul wanted to *fully know* his Saviour.

Paul was so controlled by love for his Lord (see 2 Cor. 5:14) that he became as an Olympic athlete running for the Master. His motive was to "press on toward the goal for the prize of the upward call of God in Christ Jesus" (Phil. 3:14). As the well-trained Greek runner strained every fiber of muscle to attain the winner's wreath, so Paul ran as a winner for Jesus. Aim! Run! Win! These three short words were the summary of Paul's efforts (see 1 Cor. 9:24-27). Because of his compassion for Christ, Paul could echo the true attitude of his heart: "I have learned to be content in whatever circumstances I am" (Phil. 4:11).

Was this some overnight revelation? Did the light bulb of truth switch on immediately? No! Note an important word repeated twice in Philippians 4:10-13. Paul says "I have *learned*" this attitude of contentment. The ingredient of *truth* was brought to bear upon Paul's experience, and the teaching process guided by the Spirit of God used these elements to develop the attitude of contentment. This same opportunity is available to each of us.

God Does Not Waste Time

As soon as Jonah hit the water the sea "stopped its raging." God's tool had completed its task. *The third point to notice is that God acts—often immediately—upon man's obedience.* Our Father delights in obedience! Even Christ Himself "learned obedience from the things which He suffered; and having been made perfect, He became to all those who obey Him the source of eternal salvation" (Heb. 5:8,9).

The privilege of the Christian is to obey Jesus Christ (see 1 Pet. 1:2) and "as obedient children, do not be conformed to the former lusts which were yours in ignorance" (1 Pet. 1:14).

It is from this attitude of obedience that those of us in the body of Christ will be able to develop a fervent love for one another (see 1 Pet. 1:22).

God Takes Out the Garbage

Sin in the believer's life can pile up like a trash heap. *The fourth observation to make is that Jonah had to leave; he was granted a special leave of absence.* God had ordained a "going-away party" for His runaway prophet!

The application is this: God's desire is that sin be cast out of our lives. We too may experience the storm of His fury as long as we continue to disobey His Word.

The old does not belong with the new. Paul instructed the believers at Corinth, "Therefore, if any man is in Christ, he is a new creature; the old things passed away; behold, new things have come" (2 Cor. 5:17). What a fantastic truth! We become a brand-new creation at the time we place our faith in Jesus Christ.

But how do we react to this new life? Sometimes like an antique dealer! We enjoy holding on to those antiques of our former way of life. They feel so good to have around; we've grown so accustomed to them!

Imagine how stupid it would have been for me to tenaciously hang on to the old battery in my '41 Dodge coupe and then put it into our new Honda car! New cars do not operate on antique batteries. Jesus said something similar to this when He related the parables of the "new patch on an old garment" and the "new wine in old wineskins" to the disobedient and nearsighted spiritual leaders of Israel (see Luke 5:36-39).

Our new life in Jesus Christ does not operate on old batteries—on our old, sinful habits. The old self with its evil practices must be *put on* (see Col. 3:1-11).

This section of Scripture is Paul's description of the believer's new "wardrobe" of spiritual qualities. The best suit in the house is mentioned in Romans 13:14. We are to "put on the Lord Jesus Christ."

The practical question is, "How does this happen?" When we let the Word of God richly dwell within our hearts (see

53

Col. 3:16), we will be equipped with the facts we need. How can we recognize the new garments of character we are to put on if we do not have the facts about them? Our privilege and responsibility as God's children is to *know the facts* from the one great fact book, the Bible!

The Fear of God

"It is calm. The clouds have parted. The waves are hushed. The heavens are beautiful and blue. Onward the strange vessel flits, beating her quiet tack, unconscious of her matchless story; but her crew aware 'that a prophet of the Lord has been among them.' "[2]

Once our focus was on Jonah, but now he is nowhere around; he is still on his way *down*, heading down into the depths of the blue Mediterranean!

Our attention is again drawn to the ship and the crew: "Then the men feared the Lord greatly, and they offered a sacrifice to the Lord and made vows" (1:16).

Three times there is fear. Jonah 1:5 says, "Then the sailors became afraid." The crew experienced the great storm and began to realize the *power of God.* In verse 10 "the men became extremely frightened" after Jonah had revealed his identity. Through this rebellious servant the sailors became aware of the *person of God.*

And now, in verse 16, these men are on the threshold of knowing the *pardon of God!* What had they witnessed? They had seen an act of obedient faith and its result—once a storm, but now a stillness. Through the events that transpired, the power, the person, and the pardon of a sovereign God had invaded the experience of these ungodly sailors.

The men "feared the Lord greatly." Their personal storm of unbelief had been quelled by the serenity of faith. God had captured their attention, earned their reverence, and confirmed their belief.

Faith Gets Busy!

We must not miss the rest of this verse: "They offered a sacrifice to the Lord and made vows." The proper *attitude of reverence* is displayed in the proper *actions of response.* More than likely there was some livestock on board this Phoenician vessel as it sailed for Tarshish. The crew grabbed one of these animals and offered a sacrifice on the deck of the ship. What a vivid picture at this very moment: Jonah is in the deep as a sacrifice of obedience, and the sailors are on deck offering a sacrifice of worship!

"They . . . made vows." Perhaps this statement refers to the sailors' covenant with God to continue their worship and praise once they returned to the land. We can see two areas of application here: Their sacrifice relates to *worship*, and their vows relate to *service.*

When each year comes to an end and the New Year's festivities begin, many people set out making a long list of resolutions for the coming 365 days. Almost everyone composes some sort of a "do better" program, written or mental.

When I was in grade school this was a yearly routine at the neighborhood Methodist church. On New Year's Eve we all went up to the front of the sanctuary and participated in communion. I had a very limited knowledge of what was going on, but I do remember that as we knelt it was time to write out our lists.

You should have seen all the areas of improvement I was about to tackle. "I'm not going to slug my sister or fight with my brother. I'm going to be a good helper for my parents and try to get good grades in school." I wrote down everything that crossed my mind.

These resolutions, along with many others, were sealed in a self-addressed envelope. Three months later I ran out to the mailbox and ripped open the envelope, only to discover that I had violated every resolution I had made!

My sting of conviction lasted about 10 minutes, and then I was off to the baseball field again. The point here is this: Resolutions or vows cannot be kept according to some sort of mechanical program of self-improvement. Any vow or covenant before God that is real is one that *first comes from a changed heart*! These sailors made their vows *after* they had placed their trust in Yahweh.

What is impressive about this verse is the order of events. Notice the sequence: They feared the Lord; they offered a sacrifice; they made vows. We often miss this. We turn the order around in our own nearsighted enthusiasm. We say, "Well, I'm going to get busy for God!" As an active student or layman we can easily cram our schedules full of good Christian activities, only to find ourselves so wrapped up in the *practice* that we forget the preliminary step of *praise*! Our *work* for God crowds out our *worship* of God.

The Lord's patience is needed to slow us down so that we can pray, praise, and worship Him! The *work* of the church will be realized only as the *worship* in the church is revitalized! *Praise* will lead to *practice*; *worship* will strengthen our *work*.

Into the Fish

What has happened to the sinking servant? As verse 17 begins, we return to the opening words of the chapter: "And the Lord." God had the first word, and now He speaks the final words. When the Lord first spoke He provided a great storm. In this final act He prepares a great fish. "And the Lord appointed a great fish to swallow Jonah, and Jonah was in the stomach of the fish three days and three nights."

Our sovereign Creator knows the end from the beginning (see Isa. 46:9-11). The fact that Jonah headed for the bottom did not surprise God. Our Lord's preparations and programs are never a last-minute effort. Was Jonah lost at sea? No! He had been lost in sin, but now God has a great fish appointed to perform a great work for Him. As the familiar expression puts it, "Men's disappointments are really God's appointments."

When I first read Jonah 1:17 I was tempted to ask God what in the world He expected to accomplish with a scaly sea monster! Then I remembered that God is in the "canning business" here! The truth that is highlighted for our understanding is that *God will faithfully preserve that which He fully possesses.*

And what did God use for that canning jar? Perhaps a white

shark. In Matthew 12:40 Jesus used a Greek word that referred to any sea monster or huge fish. Some Bible interpreters think this sea monster was a sperm whale. But whatever genus and species it was, this container was specifically prepared for Jonah; its wide mouth was ready and the Lord's sealing process was set.

Exactly how did God do this? I don't know. But I do know that a miracle-working God displayed His love toward a man who had turned his back and run. The fact to remember is that God did not create some sea monster at this moment, but He had this creature prepared ahead of time for use at this precise spot in the sea!

No Heroes Required

Have you ever thought that in order to be used by God you would have to become a great person? Perhaps you felt that the requirement for effective service was being "up front" as a teacher, missionary, professor, author or pastor.

Well, wipe out those erroneous ideas! God has only one requirement—a willing heart. If you're feeling blue about not being used by the Lord, maybe it is due to a life that is too concerned with self-glory. The exhortation is clear in this concluding verse. God can even use a fish to carry out His glorious purposes!

At times we become spiritual hero-worshipers. The men and women listed in God's "hall of faith" (see Heb. 11) were ordinary people like you and me. They were not superhuman. But *they did entrust their lives to a supernatural God.*

To me, the most encouraging part of Hebrews 11 is verse 40, "Because God had provided something better for us." Our privilege as Christians should catapult us out of despair and bring the sunshine of delight into our lives! You and I are trophies of God's grace! Certainly we will have different abilities and talents and opportunities, but each of us is great in God's eyes. Think of it—you are so valuable to God that He invested the life of His only Son to redeem you and draw you to Himself. Greatness lies in the fact of *who you are* and not in *what you have,* or in *what you do.*

God's Prepared Fish

God's prepared fish swallowed Jonah to *save* him, not to *silence* him. It swallowed him to preserve the prophet, not to put away his life.

The critics often get excited when we come to verse 17. "There is no fish or whale that's capable of doing that!" they cry. On the basis of this one verse, some people are prepared to toss the entire story of Jonah out of the biblical record. What really bothers them is that this whole whale incident might be just a fanciful farce. "God wouldn't lower Himself to use some creature that just happened to float along at this moment."

Some amazing theories have been offered to deny the historical validity of the account. One person said that as Jonah was floundering in the water another ship came by and rescued him. The name of that vessel was "The Whale"! Another fabrication was that as Jonah was struggling in the sea at the point of drowning, the carcass of a dead whale came floating by, so Jonah crawled inside and was later found alive!

When we turn to Matthew 12, the Lord Jesus Christ helps us to confirm the certainty of the historical record. The context is Jesus' reply to the scribes and Pharisees who had provoked Him to give them some sort of sign. His reply was right to the point: "An evil and adulterous generation craves for a sign; and yet no sign shall be given to it but the sign of Jonah the prophet; for just as Jonah was three days and three nights in the belly of the sea-monster; so shall the Son of Man be three days and three nights in the heart of the earth" (Matt. 12:39,40).

Would our Lord use this occasion to be facetious? Hardly. Rather, He spoke of a true, historical incident which pictured His own upcoming burial in the tomb. If Jesus certified the accuracy of the record, then it is clear that the verse should remain unchallenged.

Numerous documented accounts are available to prove that this event was not contrary to the laws of nature. I would encourage you to read some of these fascinating stories.[3] But while the critics joke and argue about the fish, let us not forget this story's significant truths relating to God's purposes.

Jonah's Spiritual Revival

At this point God is still in the process of preparing Jonah for his preaching mission to Nineveh. God did not forget His Word, nor did He forget the great work that needed to be done in that "Singapore of the East"!

Jonah was being tailor-made for the job. Before he was ready to preach any message, he needed a spiritual revival.

The application is clear to us. Before we can witness, before we can effectively serve in the name of the Lord, we need to be swallowed too. God needs to "swallow" us by His grace!

Hebrews 12 teaches us that God has a divine plan for disciplining His children. As He puts us through the paces, it is not a particularly enjoyable experience: "All discipline for the moment seems not to be joyful, but sorrowful; yet to those who have been trained by it, afterwards it yields the peaceful fruit of righteousness" (Heb. 12:11).

This is not a process of *punishment* but one of *perfection*. God's spiritual spankings help develop a godly character in us—one that radiates God's own nature (see Heb. 12:10).

What do you think Jonah was doing down in that dark chamber? He was taking a three-day spiritual retreat! He turned that watery prison into a prayer room! Surely Jonah needed this precious time to ponder, to pray and to praise his great God.

Have you heard of the "upper room" (see John 13)? Well, this is the "inner room"! Three days and three nights was the duration of Jonah's retreat. According to Jewish usage, "three days and three nights" was an idiom. *Any part* of a day or night was counted as a full day or night. See instances of this in 1 Samuel 20:12; Esther 4:16; and Matthew 12:40.[4] This three-day "time out" allowed Jonah to reflect on the grace and glory of God.

All of us need times of spiritual refreshment. When was the last time you were alone with your wife or husband—I mean *really alone*? This is such a badly neglected area. Why not take a special "love retreat" just by yourselves? No children, no pets, no obligations—just the two of you together!

Sound impossible? Look at your calendar today and ask God to give you that special day or weekend for your getaway. Make arrangements ahead of time for the children. When Lynn and I have done this, it seemed as if we were stepping out into a new honeymoon.

If your spiritual spark is at a low ebb, maybe this idea is for you. You need time by yourselves to plan, to dream, to talk, to be quiet, to sort out the details and events that come whirling your way in the fast-paced life-style of our time.

No Strain for the Brain

Not only was there a *spiritual revival* in the heart of Jonah, but there was also a *re-alignment* going on as well! The prophet's mental watchfulness got straightened out so he could again see God's viewpoint. Jonah's focus was getting readjusted; he was again beginning to see God's mind.

Our distorted thinking can only be re-aligned by God Himself. Paul wrote a rather strong and precise exhortation to the Roman Christians when he said, "I urge you, therefore, brethren, by the mercies of God, to present your bodies a living and holy sacrifice, acceptable to God, which is your spiritual service of worship. And do not be conformed to this world, but be transformed by the renewing of your mind, that you may prove what the will of God is, that which is good and acceptable and perfect" (Rom. 12:1,2).

Phillips' paraphrase brings the meaning right up to date: "Don't let the world around you squeeze you into its own mold, but let God remold your minds from within."

What is the key to avoiding this big squeeze? It is found in the word "renewing." The original text uses a unique word that means a renewal or restoration. Only one other New Testament passage (see Titus 3:5) has this exact word, and the idea that is involved is a spiritual process of inner remodeling. The Holy Spirit through the Word of God goes to work on the inside. This is not just another outward whitewash job; this is an inner transformation of the real me—my whole mental faculty.

60

The word that Paul uses to describe this change or meta-morphosis that is invisible to the naked eye is "transformed." Paul also writes in 2 Corinthians 3:18 that as we behold the glory of the Lord we "are being transformed into the same image from glory to glory." Imagine the privilege we have as God's child. As we read and study and memorize God's living Word, we are being remolded into the very image of Jesus Christ!

"Is it important to spend time in the Bible?" How should we answer that question? A long argument or speech is un-necessary; the answer is clearly yes! Not only is it *important*, but it is absolutely *essential*. We cannot grow to be like Christ apart from knowing the way through God's Word.

Our own perspective on living, on housework, on our jobs, or on our leisure time often gets fuzzy. We need God's view-point in every aspect of our living or we easily become frus-trated. It's not just a matter of having a head jammed full of Bible verses and facts, but a heart that is open to *respond* to that truth.

Preserving the Preacher

Jonah's physical walk had now been restored. Had God abandoned His mission for Nineveh? Not in any way! Nor had He given up on Jonah. God made sure that His man would be ready for the job He had assigned him.

Jonah's deep-sea experience prefigures the death and burial of Jesus Christ (see Matt. 12:40; 27:63ff). The most dramatic historical moments the universe has ever known—the death, burial, and resurrection of the Son of God—are partially de-picted by a disciplined prophet in the stomach of a sea mon-ster! How can we fathom the mind of God? "But God has chosen the foolish things of the world to shame the wise, and God has chosen the weak things of the world to shame the things which are strong" (1 Cor. 1:27).

God was vitally interested in preserving the body of His Son. Remember, as John describes it in 19:31-42 of his Gos-pel, that faithful women continued to minister to the body of Jesus. The Jewish custom of preparation with potent spices was applied to His body. Even Nicodemus got into the picture; he came bearing the hundred pounds of spices (see v. 39) for Jesus' burial. Had his heart been changed by this crucified Galilean?

Why is all this important? Because the preparation, the burial wrappings, and the spices all relate to the importance of Christ's *body*. The *life* and the *body* of Jesus were inseparably involved in God's mission. It was this same body (resurrected) that was to soon appear before a skeptical Thomas (see John 20:26-29).

It was this same body that bore the slash mark of a Roman spear and the gashing holes of wooden spikes. The very *body* of Jesus was an inescapable testimony of the grace of a sovereign God! That same body had a mission—to appear before 500 people at one time (see 1 Cor. 15:6) and to accompany the two men on the road to Emmaus (see Luke 24:13ff).

The psalmist said, "Neither wilt thou suffer thine Holy One to see corruption" (Ps. 16:10, *KJV*). *God will faithfully preserve that which He fully possesses.*

Does all this seem historically remote? This same Jesus in His glorified body will be the matchless sight before our eyes when we see Him face-to-face! He will be there to welcome us home in His glorified *body*.

Jonah had a mission still ahead of him. He needed a body; he needed a vehicle through which God could proclaim His message of mercy!

The prophet Jonah had now given everything into the hand of his God; he gave all of himself. And now God finally had all of Jonah, and He preserved him for a great future ministry.

Think back with me to the scene atop Mount Moriah (see Gen. 22). A knife was raised in midair and a beloved son was upon the altar of sacrifice. What raced through Isaac's mind as his father stood poised with that gleaming blade of steel?

As Abraham's muscles were ready for the downward swing, "the angel of the Lord called to him from heaven. [Stop! Do not touch him!] Now I know that you fear God, since you have not withheld your son, your only son, from Me" (Gen. 22:11, 12).

62

In that moment, Abraham had fully surrendered his own will to that of Yahweh. His trust was complete; God had all of Abraham. Isaac was preserved, and a substitute was provided for the offering.

Dead or Alive?

Scholars disagree about Jonah 1:17. Did Jonah die? The text says that Jonah was gulped down; it nowhere states that he died. God preserved him alive! Some may contend that in order for Jonah to be a true picture of Christ's death, burial, and resurrection, he had to really die. But this reasoning is not correct. Nor was Jonah to be truly resurrected. Jesus Christ Himself is the firstfruits (see 1 Cor. 15:20-24). The only man to die as a sacrifice at God's command was Jesus, His beloved Son. *Preservation* is the correct concept.

As we close the curtain on act one of this biblical drama, we find a new appreciation for our brother Jonah. Instead of being the "greatest fish story ever told," we gain a glimpse into the very glory of our sovereign Creator!

The dominating theme in this first chapter is man's refusal to obey God. No matter how sophisticated our acts of rebellion, whether blatant or bland, the results are the same: We go down into frustration, guilt, and compounded misery. Jonah's story is our story; his struggles are our struggles!

God desires our *response*, not our *refusal*. *Obedience* is what pleases God.

GOD WILL FAITHFULLY PRESERVE
THAT WHICH HE FULLY POSSESSES.

Footnotes

1. E.B. Pusey, "Jonah" in *Barnes on the Old Testament, The Minor Prophets a Commentary*, vol. 1 (Grand Rapids: Baker Book House, 1973), p. 406.
2. Hugh Martin, *The Prophet Jonah* (London: Banner of the Truth Trust, 1966), p. 185.
3. Some very intriguing and well-documented accounts of the swallowing of human beings by large fish are cited by Gleason Archer, p. 302 (note 8); Frank Gaebelein, pp. 88-97; J. Vernon McGee, pp. 18-20; Ven. Perowne, pp. 92,93. See Bibliography for titles.
4. E.W. Bullinger, *Figures of Speech Used in the Bible* (Grand Rapids: Baker Book House, 1968), pp. 845-847.

7 | Voice from the Deep
Jonah 2:1–4

Why don't I pray more? Why don't you? Is it due to a crammed schedule? Am I not being spiritually sensitive? These are haunting questions for many of us.

If these convicting, frustrating questions are troubling you, take heart! We have come to the place where God has fashioned Jonah into a man of prayer. Let us discover together some great principles of prayer from this unusual man in an unusual prayer closet.

We will be entering into the "inner parts" of the great fish. Jonah is about to demonstrate to us some basic principles of effective prayer. Let's climb in and see how we can develop an effective prayer life!

As we open the Bible to Jonah 2:1-4, we want to note two significant points: *What* Jonah is praying and *how* Jonah is praying.

Prayer of the Deep

A great God had sent a great storm and had appointed a great fish to teach His runaway servant. After leaving the decks of a Phoenician vessel sailing to Tarshish, Jonah headed down into the deep for a three-day retreat in solitary confinement!

"Then Jonah prayed to the Lord his God from the stomach of the fish" (2:1). Though the motley bunch of sailors captured much of our attention in Jonah chapter 1, now we hear a prayer from the lips of Jonah himself. This is not like the awe-filled cry to the Lord that passed from the sailors' lips, for Jonah's prayer consisted of deep bursts of praise from one who had been conquered by God's grace.

Notice that this is the first time in the book that Jonah prays. How could he have time to pray when he was hotfooting it away from God? It's hard to pray to the God you're running from!

The very first verse of Jonah chapter 2 strikes the weakest area of our spiritual lives. So often we come home overloaded with precious truths and spiritual nuggets from a group Bible study or sermon message. We may even be excited about the privilege and responsibility of talking with our heavenly Father in prayer!

But when the clock strikes the bedtime hour we curl up under those clean, white sheets and manage to shoot up a five-minute "quickie" prayer. Here it is 11 P.M., and we're struggling to keep our heavy eyelids from drooping shut. "But, Lord, I'm praying! Can't you hear me?"

From his watery closet, Jonah offers a prayer of thanksgiving. It is a very personal communication directed to "the Lord my God." Some Bible critics say that this prayer was inserted here to give Jonah a new image, to make him look good. Others contend that Jonah was so overwhelmed in getting ejected from that watery compartment of the fish's belly that he wrote this thank-you prayer to the Lord.

But when we examine the content of this psalm-prayer, we find the answer to the critics' protest. Dr. Edward J. Young has given us the proper perspective in his *Introduction to the Old Testament.* He clearly shows that Wellhausen and other objectors to the genuineness of Jonah 2:2-9 misinterpret the meaning of the psalm completely. Says Young: "This is *not* a psalm of thanksgiving *for deliverance from a whale's belly.* It is rather a psalm of thanksgiving *for deliverance from drowning.* The figures of speech employed in this psalm have reference to drowning, not to a whale's belly."[1]

Memories of Deliverance

Never had Jonah turned to the Lord during the violent gale, but now he utters his heart's song of deliverance. When did he pray? As he entered the fish? The vivid imagery is highly descriptive and would lend itself to this position. However, what we have here is the record of Jonah's prayer written down after he had been miraculously returned to dry land.

Jonah recalls with heightened sensitivity every detail of his near-drowning experience! Men rescued from the sea have recounted stories of their quickened consciousness in the face of drowning. The adrenalin must have really been pumping throughout Jonah's body!

Since Jonah did not bring along his writing tablet while he was sloshing around in those darkened quarters, this is a recollection of his heart's thoughts and yearnings while in confinement. This is truly "communication in confinement"; what else could he do?

How often do you stop to praise and worship God in prayer for all that He has done? If you are in the process of running away from the Lord, then I imagine your prayer life is pretty pathetic—boring, stale and meaningless.

When the kids, the dog, and the doorbell are making pandemonium of our palace, it's tough to find a moment of quiet solitude for prayer. In Jonah's day it was no different. In fact, with greater affluence we have greater distractions. Maybe that is why God had to tear Jonah away from everything and confine him to the quietest place in the sea!

What does Jonah say? "I called out of my distress to the Lord, and He answered me. I cried out for help from the depth of Sheol" (2:2).

I don't know whether Jonah prayed audibly or with a silent call of the heart, and it doesn't really matter, since his inner life was being communicated to the Father. Psalm 139:4 says, "Even before there is a word on my tongue, behold, O Lord, Thou dost know it all."

God heard Jonah! He is always ready to listen. From any spot on the face of the earth there is equal access to the throne of heaven. No one person or no special place can claim greater status in communicating with God.

Jonah cries out to Yahweh with an intense prayer. These were the same words used by the sailors in 1:14. This prayerful cry emerges "out of my distress." This literally means that

66

he's calling out to the Lord from the very predicament that God had placed him into.

Being tucked away in a sea creature's belly isn't what I would call a very scintillating experience, and Jonah is tumbling around in gastric juices, praying! From this gross compartment he cries out "from the depth of Sheol," from the "belly" of hell. Jonah's language is filled with Hebrew imagery. He does not mean the literal hell that we think of in the teachings of the New Testament. In this passage the word "Sheol" is used in the figurative sense of a grave or the underworld.[2] This is the place of no escape; it is the last stop of Jonah's downward path away from the presence of the Lord. The final juncture in his flight from God is this coffin of confinement.

Two times in verse 2 there is a gleam of light that pierces the darkness: "And He answered me . . . . Thou didst hear my voice." Even here God can hear! From desolate ends of the earth the Father listens for the cry of His own.

The Pit of Hell

Do you remember the phrase from the movie, *The Hiding Place*? Corrie ten Boom, after having undergone tremendous physical and emotional persecution at the hands of the German Nazis at Ravensbruck concentration camp, realized that she was "in the pit of hell itself."

As her sovereign and loving Lord began to break through her own bitterness and hatred, and after seeing the reality of faith in her sister Betsie, Corrie was delivered from the jaws of death. The statement she made and realized in reflection has jogged my mind ever since: "There is no pit that is deep, but that His love is deeper still!" Oh, how great is the love of God for us!

What a faith-builder! Imagine, even Sheol itself is under God's sovereign control! God heard Jonah and answered. God hears you from the pit of your predicament, and *He will answer you!*

We are so quick to memorize Psalm 66:18: "If I regard wickedness in my heart, the Lord will not hear." We need to understand the truth of this. But why stop there? Look at what follows in context: "But certainly God has heard; He has given heed to the voice of my prayer. Blessed be God, who has not turned away my prayer, nor His lovingkindness from me" (Ps. 66:19,20).

As we proceed to verse 3, Jonah has an opportune time to really let someone have it! Right here he could have vented any pent-up feelings of revenge. But what does he pray? "For *Thou* hadst cast me into the deep."

Jonah does not put the blame on anyone, but admits that God is in control. He realizes that the sailors carried out the sovereign will of the Lord. It was God behind it all, right from the beginning.

This very word "deep" is used in the book of Exodus. Remember how the children of Israel, in their flight from Pharaoh, witnessed a miracle on the banks of the Red Sea? The great waves parted and Moses led the nation across on dry ground.

But Pharaoh was fast on their heels. His army of thundering chariots sped down the hillside and out onto the dry seabed. But the hand of God moved nature again, and the waters returned and closed in upon the Egyptians, consuming their whole army in the deep. Exodus 15:5 says, "The deeps covered them"; Pharaoh's henchmen sunk like rocks into the depths! This was no shallow creek; the waters covered an entire army, and they all drowned.

Jonah says that he was cast "into the heart of the seas, and the current engulfed me." It is almost as if God reached down and opened a zippered pocket right in the middle of the waters and plunked Jonah right inside!

The word "seas" is plural. I wonder why? Perhaps this is an indication by the Spirit of God to alert us to the fact of Jonah's absolute helplessness. He was dumped into the heart of the seas, into the middle of a vast body of water. The plurality of the word suggests the insurmountable odds that he faced.

Do We Need Props?

I must admit that I haven't been in that position very often.

Have you? Perhaps we need more instances like Jonah's—maybe not in water, but in situations in which God casts us into a place of real helplessness, where our only recourse is to fall completely and totally upon our Lord. Dependence means survival!

My response is usually something like this: "Okay, Lord, I'm ready. I've got my scuba gear on . . . everything is go!"

"Son, you won't need that equipment. Let's take it off."

"Well, if you insist, Lord, that's all right with me."

"Are you ready now?"

"Yes, Sir! Do you have my hand?"

"No. I'm not even going to hold your hand."

"Really? Well, okay. But I'm sure you have the life jacket right there, don't you?"

"No. Not even a life jacket. Nothing!"

"Oh, no! Nothing? I mean—not even a rope? How about an old inner tube, Lord?"

"Nothing."

We fight for any prop of stability to "keep us afloat." It is these props that keep us from our total dependence upon God's adequate care. And look at the beautiful props we have: money, health, a good job, nice friends, status, reputation, and many others. Oh, the props aren't bad; it's just that they too easily become our life-support system!

Jonah Had No Props

God placed Jonah into a helpless position. He was assigned to a spot in the heart of the great sea, so that even his clever, creative and courageous human abilities were utterly useless! It was only then that God broke through!

The text reads, "And the current engulfed me. All thy breakers and billows passed over me." The *KJV* reads "the floods compassed me." The literal translation means to be completely surrounded, closed in, encompassed. There was nothing Jonah could do—nothing! Even if he had taken a crash course at the local YMCA pool in Red Cross lifesaving techniques, he could not have won the battle of the blue.

Jonah continues in verse 4, "So I said, 'I have been expelled from Thy sight.' Nevertheless I will look again toward Thy holy temple!" Had God driven out this prophet from before His eyes? No! Jonah had ripped himself away from God's loving care as he acted in disobedience. In reflection and meditation he sees how costly that move was. To escape from personal fellowship with God leaves only an empty desperation.

"I will look again." Jonah's desire and hope echoed the very words of Moses in Exodus 3. As God revealed Himself through the burning bush, "Moses hid his face, for he was afraid to look at God" (Exod. 3:6). What a magnificent moment of humility!

At this point we see a magnificent act of faith. Jonah proclaims that he will look intently, with a fixed vision of expectation, "toward Thy holy temple." Recall the words of Psalm 121, one of the hymns that the Jews sang as they made their pilgrimage up to Jerusalem and the Temple.

"I will lift up my eyes to the mountains; from whence shall my help come? My help comes from the Lord, who made heaven and earth. He will not allow your foot to slip; He who keeps you will not slumber. Behold, He who keeps Israel will neither slumber nor sleep" (Ps. 121:1-4).

What was Jonah saying at this point on the brink of death? He did not know what was ahead, but he thanked God for saving him from such a lonely, horrible death by drowning.

"Father, I don't know what lies around the corner for me, or even in the next few moments, but I will continue to look to You! Even right here, in this gloomy cell, I will look to You by faith. No matter what happens, Lord, You will fill my vision." What trust! What a declaration! Pusey says, "What he could not do in the body, he would do in his soul. This was his only resource."[3]

Having seen a brief overview of these opening verses of Jonah's prayer, let's go back and retrieve some valuable, practical principles of prayer. There are a number of classic prayers recorded in the Scriptures, and this is one of them. Note these prayer hints for our instruction.

The Privilege of Prayer

"Then Jonah prayed" (2:1). This is the first time that we have a recorded prayer of the prophet Jonah. He had turned from his privileged access to God when he ran away; everything focused on his disobedience. But now Jonah wants to get back on God's wavelength; he realizes the precious privilege he had shunned.

Of the 12 Hebrew words used for prayer, Jonah selects a word that speaks about the *objective idea* of prayer. It is the same word that is used of Hannah's utterance in 1 Samuel 2:1-10.[4]

Phillips Brooks said that "prayer is not the overcoming of God's reluctance, it is the taking hold of God's willingness." Prayer is indeed a privilege for every believer. "Let us therefore draw near with confidence to the throne of grace, that we may receive mercy and may find grace to help in time of need" (Heb. 4:16).

Let us be rescued from a sloppy attitude of communion with our heavenly Father; direct access to Him through Jesus Christ is a coveted privilege! (See especially Rom. 8:26,27,34; 1 Tim. 2:5.)

The Direction of Prayer

Prayer is to be directed to God. Its focus is to be godward to the Father: "Jonah prayed to the Lord his God." The belly of the great fish was not filled with the random mutterings of a grateful heart, but was filled instead with a stream of praise and thanksgiving that made its way unto Yahweh, Jonah's Elohim!

This title *Elohim* emphasizes the creatorship of God, His sovereign control of nature and His power that sustains all living things.

"In the beginning God created the heavens and the earth" (Gen. 1:1) The very first verse of our Bible uses the designation Elohim.[5] Jonah addressed his personal Lord, his God who is the divine Creator and Controller of all life.

It is interesting to observe that in the recorded prayers of Jesus Christ, He addresses His Father on nearly every occasion. The only time Jesus omitted the word Father was in His cry from the cross: "My God, My God, why hast Thou forsaken Me?" (see Mark 15:34; Matt. 27:46). This statement is taken from Psalm 22:1, in which the translation for God is Elohim.

The Place of Prayer

The principle Jonah demonstrated here is that we can pray from anywhere. Even the inward parts of a Mediterranean fish cannot clog the channels of prayer!

Certainly this fact should shatter a few of our spiritual misconceptions—like the one which insists upon praying from only one spot! "Lord, I just can't pray unless I kneel in the prayer room behind the church platform. I can't really talk with you unless I pray at my routine time, in my routine manner, and according to my routine method."

These statements are a bit strained, but they do capture some of our erroneous attitudes about prayer. Jonah did not have these options. Nevertheless, he realized the privilege of his personal communion with the Lord and directed his life unto the God who loved him and was sovereign over his actions.

Location is not important, but *the longing of the heart is!* Jonah prayed right there from the fish's belly!

The Postion of Prayer

Do you think Jonah was kneeling in the belly of the great fish? Though we can't know for sure, more than likely he was in a twisted knot, upside down and backwards!

In those early days of my walk with Jesus Christ I had a number of well-meaning saints point out that the Christian's prayer position was to be found on one's knees. Great stories were told about how this famous missionary or that godly pastor would arise at 4 A.M. and "hit the floor on his knees" in prayer for two or three hours.

So I tried this method for a few mornings, but that's about all! After several minutes on my kneecaps my body was wracked in pain. No longer did I have my heart set upon God.

What I have come to appreciate is the fact that God does not put His mark of approval upon the position of our *bodies*, but upon the position of our *hearts*. Our attitude in prayer, our concentration upon God's Person and work, is far more significant then grinding out 10 minutes on aching knees just to be proper.

The Scriptures frequently indicate that people knelt in humble prayer before God. In Gethsemane our Lord not only fell to His knees, He went all the way down upon His face (see Matt. 26:39).

You may find yourself praying with open eyes as you drive along the freeway. (Please don't get into the habit of closing your eyes while behind the wheel!) As requests for prayer are shared with me, I will take a few minutes seated at my desk to bring that need before the Father.

If we are faithful in learning to "pray without ceasing" (1 Thess. 5:17), there will be countless opportunities to pray in a variety of positions. Prayer is positionless!

The Intensity of Prayer

The comments of William Law about our fervency in prayer are deeply convicting: "It is not the arithmetic of our prayers, how many they are; not the rhetoric of our prayers, how sweet our voice may be; not the logic of our prayers, how argumentative they may be; not the method of our prayers, how orderly they may be—which God cares for. Fervency of spirit is that which availeth much."[6]

Jonah called out, cried out to his God. He was in no shape to be petty or careless! Why are we so formal in our intimate communion with God? Our prayers are but whispered mechanical ditties that neither reflect our needs nor move God to act. This is not always the case, but too often it is. Perhaps the schedule of our busy days crowds out a quiet, meditative time alone with the Lord.

Our object should not be to have some emotional explosion every time we address the Father, but as we bring together our mind, heart and will in harmony with His presence and open up the channels of honest, personal communication with our God, then prayer becomes a dynamic experience and not a dull exercise.

Prayer need not, should not, be a monotony; it should be a meaningful part of our relationship with Christ.

The Predicament of Prayer

From where do we pray? From *any* predicament in which we find ourselves. Jonah called to the Lord out of his affliction and distress. God does not expect or desire us to be "Pepsodent" Christians, only coming to Him with smiling white teeth when everything is just peachy!

Near our home a neighbor's driveway contained a shallow area that usually remained filled with muddy water. If you can picture our son Matthew—an energetic, restless body with a crop of red-blonde hair—you know exactly the place where he headed as soon as he came running out the front door: right to the puddle!

One of his favorite games was called "Splash." The technique was simple: Grab a dead branch from a tree and beat the puddle until the mud and water went flying everywhere! To make this game a bit more exciting, Matthew would often wade into the middle of the water and squat down. Head, hair, hands, face, clothes—not an inch was missed!

Just about this time, when Matt's tree branch was sending torrents of mud and water in every direction, I would appear on the horizon driving our VW bug. Matt would spot that familiar object and come tearing across the yard. "Daddy's home! Daddy's home!"

Of course I enjoyed every bit of this response, but my boy looked like some brown blob out of the local horror movie. What was so precious was his excited response to me, his dad. Not even the mud stopped him; he called to me right from the middle of the puddle. He didn't care what he looked like, but he did show his concern for our relationship.

How could I help but respond? Many times I would enter the house with mud splotches all over my clothes from having put my arms around him.

Let's get away from our distorted way of thinking which dictates that before we can come to the Father everything has to be just so—a sinless life, wrongs confessed, and everything in tip-top shape!

Our Father longs to respond when we're hurting, when sin has tackled us to the turf, when we're sick of our ways. He can see through that mud to the longing heart beneath.

The Anticipation of Prayer

Effective prayer anticipates a response. Notice the words in verse 2: "And He answered me....Thou didst hear my voice."

Having been delivered from death, David says in Psalm 116:4, "Then I called upon the name of the Lord: 'O Lord, I beseech Thee, save my life!'"

When we really know someone is listening, we are apt to pray with a greater sensitivity and anticipation of response. Repeatedly, Lynn has told me something two or three times, only to have my grunt of response quickly forgotten as I went off and neglected her need. I say this to my shame, because poor listening does not develop anticipation; it develops apathy instead.

What an opportunity to cultivate anticipation in our local church body! As we listen and seek to meet needs, the greater will be the willingness to share those needs.

The application to our prayer life is clear: As we recognize that God *really is listening*, that He hears the cries from our hearts, then we will wait with grateful anticipation for His perfect response.

The Scope of Prayer

Effective prayer recognizes the sovereignty of God. All of life and all circumstances we encounter are either caused or allowed to happen according to the will of God.

Notice Jonah's particular phrases in verse 3: "*Thou* hadst cast me....all *Thy breakers*—" (italics added). God is behind it all. The proper scope of prayer sees a mighty God. We must recognize the scope of our God—infinite and sovereign!

From the greatest problems to the smallest, God is sovereign and sincerely concerned.

Effective prayer recognizes God's hand in everything, the major and the minor.

The Language of Prayer

Notice the language that Jonah uses. Much of his prayer is filled with selected materials from the Psalms; the language is biblical.

When we take into account the context of the story, we discover some beautiful insight into our prayerful prophet. Even as Jonah had once turned *from* God, he is now turning *to* God. What flows out of his heart is not some contrived thesis of syllabic nonsense, but feelings which fill his heart. It is the language of the Word of God.

In the New Testament, Jesus made a very profound comment in exhorting the blasphemous spiritual leaders. He was in no position to beat around the bush as He said, "You brood of vipers, how can you, being evil, speak what is good? For the mouth speaks out of that which fills the heart" (Matt. 12:34).

The mouth is the doorway into our hearts. Pressed to the wall in godly discipline, Jonah utters forth the precious words of God that had been lodged in his heart.

In Nehemiah 1:5-11 we read of another classic prayer in the Bible. Here is a cupbearer who becomes a construction boss! Yet look at the Scripture that fills his sensitive prayer in behalf of his people.

How much we should profit from this example of "hiding the Word in the heart" (see Ps. 119)! Not only will God's truth do its purifying work in us (see Ps. 119:9), but it will enrich our communion with God in prayer.

The Humility of Prayer

Effective prayer recognizes personal sin. Jonah clearly echoes this: "For Thou hadst cast *me* into the deep . . . . *I* have been expelled from Thy sight." Jonah accepts his guilt in being a castaway from God.

Note an interesting parallel in 1 Corinthians 9. Paul speaks of disciplining his body so that he can win the race in his own Christian ministry. He says in effect (v. 27) that he does not want to become a discarded believer. Disqualification to some lesser position is not his bag; Paul wants to be God's best ambassador.

It was this driving faith that later had to contend with a "thorn in the flesh," a physical impairment that kept Paul from exalting himself. The apostle could then say in 2 Corinthians 12:9,10, "And He has said to me, 'My grace is sufficient for you, for power is perfected in weakness.' Most gladly, therefore, I will rather boast about my weaknesses, that the power of Christ may dwell in me. Therefore I am well content with weaknesses, with insults, with distresses, with persecutions, with difficulties, for Christ's sake; for when I am weak, then I am strong." Paul adds in 1 Timothy 1:15,16, "It is a trustworthy statement, deserving full acceptance, that Christ Jesus came into the world to save sinners, among whom I am foremost of all. And yet for this reason I found mercy, in order that in me as the foremost, Jesus Christ might demonstrate His perfect patience, as an example for those who would believe in Him for eternal life."

God has a unique way of taking "big shots" and showing them that they are really nothing but play bullets in His hands (see John 15:5)! Perhaps Jonah was thinking himself to be "Mr. Big Man" in the ministry until the fish made short work of that inflated ego.

God especially listens to the contrite heart. A "publican's prayer" should be our guideline (Luke 18:13).

True humility is not earned in any sort of merit system; a humble attitude will be cultivated in a life that sees the holy character of God in contrast to the sinful nature of man.

The Hope of Prayer

The last phrase in verse 4 contains a tremendous declaration of hope: "Nevertheless I will look again toward Thy holy temple."

"Whatever the cost, I will continue to trust in God." That's what Jonah is saying. Hope is always wedded to a trustworthy object.

Walking by faith is not walking by sight (2 Cor. 5:7). While we will continue to have testings and tribulations in the Christian life (2 Cor. 4:16-18; Phil. 1:29,30), the *hope* of our walk is not in the surrounding circumstances of pain but in the unseen God who is developing our character through the hurts and bruises.

Paul states this truth in Romans 5:3-5: "And not only this, but we also exult in our tribulations; knowing that tribulation brings about perseverance; and perseverance, proven character; and proven character, hope; and hope does not disappoint; because the love of God has been poured out within our hearts through the Holy Spirit who was given to us." The loving God in whom our hope is placed never lets us down!

Jonah was seeing how trustworthy the Lord really is. Love "hopes all things" (1 Cor. 13:7). It gives the benefit of the doubt; it looks ahead to a good conclusion and never leaves one dangling. Hope is positive. Hope is creative. Hope is excitingly real!

Let's Start Praying!

Armed with a few principles of effective prayer, we can become mighty before the throne of grace. As the Lord begins to work these effective principles of prayer into our lives, our "hotline to God" will become more effective than the Bell telephone system!

Do you have a specific "prayer project" that the Lord has placed before you, perhaps in the area of spiritual leadership, or submission in your marriage, or finances, or a friend's salvation? Whatever the yearnings of your heart, let the grace of God fill your life with godly prayer!

Our prayers become truly powerful when we remember that

EFFECTIVE PRAYER IS GUIDED
BY GODLY PRINCIPLES.

Footnotes

1. Edward J. Young, *An Introduction to the Old Testament* (Grand Rapids: Eerdmans, 1949), p. 257.
2. *Sheol* represents the locality or condition of the departed. The *King James Version* translates *sheol* by the words "hell," "grave," or the "pit"; the Septuagint usually renders it as "hades." There is no reason to doubt that what the grave or pit is to the *body*, *Sheol* is to the soul. It is the netherworld, and perhaps this would be the best rendering for the word. Not in one single passage is it used in the sense of the place of punishment.
3. E.B. Pusey, "Jonah," in *Barnes on the Old Testament, The Minor Prophets a Commentary*, vol. 1 (Grand Rapids: Baker Book House, 1973), p. 409.
4. Note Robert Baker Girdlestone's discussion of the 12 Hebrew words for *prayer* in *Synonyms of the Old Testament* (Grand Rapids: Eerdmans, 1974), pp. 219,220.
5. Additional information on the great name *Elohim* can be found in Botterweck, *Theological Dictionary of the Old Testament*, vol. 2, pp. 267-284; see also Girdlestone, *Synonymns of the Old Testament*, pp. 18-24. (See details in Bibliography.)
6. William Law, as quoted in J. Sidlow Baxter, *Explore the Book* (Grand Rapids: Zondervan Publishing House, 1952), p. 236.

8 | How to Be Miserable Without Even Trying
Jonah 2:5–8

A few months ago I decided to surprise Lynn. I had my secretary call a nearby Stretch and Sew shop and enroll my wife in a basic sewing course. The baby-sitting was arranged so that she could have the morning hours free to launch out on this new adventure. That evening at dinner, when I proudly revealed the secret plans, she nearly jumped off her chair with excitement!

The class was challenging and fun. As Lynn brought projects home to work on, the sewing machine was in constant motion. Patterns, stitching, and thread were the main topics of conversation.

With practice comes progressing skills, and Lynn soon "graduated" to some of the more advanced patterns. One night while she was working industriously at the machine, materials were heaped everywhere. After a few hours Lynn dejectedly held up a new pair of beautiful blue slacks. The only trouble with her product was that she had sewed two left legs together!

"Honey, what am I doing wrong? I've followed the manual and looked at my class notes and everything, but look at this mess!"

I couldn't help but look absolutely puzzled. Her disappointment was shattering. Lynn was trying to repeat a complicated process she had just seen demonstrated in class, but it wasn't coming out the way she wanted.

"This is hopeless. I can't learn this!"

After a late-night session of ripping out the seams and

backing up to the place where the mistake had been made, we finally finished the slacks!

Are You Frustrated?

Have you ever been in a frustrated, hopeless position? Perhaps you're not a seamstress, but you enjoy putting models together or trying out tantalizing new recipes or engaging in creative repair work around the house.

Do you remember arriving at that point of utter frustration? You did the very best you knew how, but still something went haywire—wrong shape, wrong size, too much, too little!

The question I would like to pose in relation to our spiritual lives is this: Why does God bring us to the point of being helpless and hopeless? What is His purpose in allowing us to go through life and coming to a place where we just throw our hands up and say, "Lord, I just don't understand this at all! What are you bringing *this* in my life for? Why me?"

In these next two chapters we will explore Jonah 2:5-10, and in this conclusion of Jonah's prayer we will discover practical insights on how to grapple with these frustrating questions. The theme of this section is a vital truth for our walk with Jesus Christ: *Effective service for God begins with a fully surrendered life.*

I'm sure Jonah didn't begin his venture away from the Lord with the burning motive of becoming miserable! But by refusing the will of God, Jonah had brought upon himself the inevitable consequences of rebellion: misery!

In verses 5-8 we see the process by which Jonah is purged of self. Chapter 9 will resume the narrative and conclude with the exciting activity of God in preparing Jonah for service.

Lord, I Am Helpless

The process of Jonah's spiritual remodeling did not begin when he entered the jaws of his scaly companion in 1:17. The process had already been underway from the moment he refused to obey the word of the Lord and headed off in the opposite direction.

That is where the process of remodeling begins for us too.

81

The moment we turn our backs on God, He seeks to turn us around.

As Jonah continues his psalm-prayer of deliverance, he seems to be crying out, "Lord, I'm helpless!" The description of his plight is painted with Hebrew imagery: "Water encompassed me to the very soul, the great deep engulfed me, weeds were wrapped around my head. I descended to the roots of the mountains. The earth with its bars was around me forever, but Thou hast brought up my life from the pit, O Lord my God" (Jon. 2:5,6).

In this personal drowning account we hear the cries of a man choking on seawater. The encircling water had overwhelmed Jonah, and his life was ready to be snuffed out.

Jonah's description is true and accurate. The greatness of the deep is in keeping with the gravity of God's discipline. The word "weed" refers to the stringy seaweeds, Jonah's grave wrappings that bound his body fast to the depths. You will recall that the technically correct name for the Red Sea is the *Reed Sea*, or Sea of Reeds. The word is the same.

What was racing through Jonah's mind at this point? The slimy seaweeds wrapped themselves around his head like a turban. These insignificant little plants on the sea floor were like chains or graveclothes.

Seaweed in Our Lives

I wonder if there are some "seaweeds" in our lives—those insignificant items that hold us back from what we truly want to do, those disturbing items that hinder our progress and distract our desires.

How do we respond to these? Jonah was responding properly, as we will shortly see. But he could have said something like this:

"Lord, look at this ugly weed! If it doesn't let go I'm done for! I'm your prophet, remember? You called me to serve you, and now I'm being tied down to my own death by this good-for-nothing plant!"

Our God uses the insignificant things in life to show us our own insignificance. He takes the small things to show us, if

82

nothing else will, that we're not as big, as clever, as important, as essential as we seem to think! Romans 12:3 says, "For through the grace given to me I say to every man among you not to think more highly of himself than he ought to think; but to think so as to have sound judgment, as God has allotted to each a measure of faith."

During my last assignment in the army I had the privilege of teaching a solid-state electronic theory course to computer students. After the basic training in theory, the men would move on to the next series of advanced classes, until they finally were able to effectively manage a large computer complex.

One afternoon a loud clatter of noise came out of the computer center, and high-echelon personnel were dashing in and out of that room all the rest of the day. When the trouble was finally diagnosed, an inexpensive component had completely fouled up a multimillion-dollar computer system! The entire array of sophisticated equipment went on the blink due to a $25.00 part.

This is similar to the "saga of the seaweed." Something small, something insignificant, is used by God to drive home to Jonah his own insignificance.

Playing in the Rain

A penetrating incident occurred in my life a few years back, and I still recall it with vivid clarity. As a sixth-grader at Longfellow Elementary School I was one of the school's "sport jocks"—a real "man-on-the-playfield" type of guy. The big event of each school day was the noon-hour soccer match. Our team boldly challenged anyone in the school to see if they could knock off the sixth-grade champions.

During our many games the competition could be so sharp that no one thought of returning to class at the sound of the bell. We were compelled to keep on playing to determine the victor. Even during rainstorms the games went on uninterrupted.

Our school principal soon learned of our antics by noticing that the hallways were beginning to look like a shower room as we traipsed back to class with pant legs dripping with water. We were kindly warned that this business must come to a halt. When we didn't comply, our dear head lady came trudging out to the playfield and literally hauled all of us back into the building.

"If you boys can't learn to come in out of that rain, perhaps you need a refresher course in obedience!" Miss Kimmel was in no mood to take any guff from us.

Not only did she give us a good lecture, but she also sent the entire team down to spend the afternoon in the kindergarten class.

Oh, the shame of it all! There we were, the hotshot six-grade guys down in the end of the school with the "babies," those insignificant little kindergartners! We sat there finger-painting, in utter humiliation.

The Lord in His sovereign way of knowing exactly what we need will allow us to have these experiences too. When self is supreme, then God's humbling process will be enforced.

Humbling Hurts

When one grows older the humbling hurts more. While at seminary in Dallas I had to learn a few more lessons in this area. I was elected the president of my first-year class. In my zeal to be helpful to my classmates I spent many hours in personal fellowship and counseling. There were a number of newly married couples that were finding the adjustments and demands of seminary life a bit rough.

All this sounded rather commendable, but the problem was that I too had just become a new Christian, and I was still in the process of trying to get my own life and recent marriage "all together." While tending to everyone else's problems and needs, I came back to our little efficiency apartment only to find my new bride frustrated and lonely. I was completely neglecting Lynn!

In bitter reflection, the Lord allowed me to see just how totally self-centered I was. A little counseling session here and another hour spent over there—little by little, bit by bit, my backward priorities soon controlled my time. While desperately attempting to be helpful toward others, I deeply wounded my wife, who should have been my first disciple!

What "seaweed" is God using in your life today? Is He utilizing something small in showing you that perhaps you are not as important as you think you are? That weed may be a person, an event, or a project—anything that God uses to show us that our greatest need is to be controlled by His Spirit. In this way He helps us maintain the right perspective on our own lives.

Down to the Bottom

Let's move on to verse 6. Jonah describes that he is going down to the very bottom or "roots" of the mountains (literally, the "cuttings off of the mountains").[1] If you have ever been on a seacoast, you know that the surrounding mountains do not come to a dead halt at the water's edge. They continue on further out underneath the water, going down and finding their roots and extremities way beyond the shore.

Jonah says that "the earth with its bars was around me forever." The walls of the sea basin became his chamber. How confining was this dungeon! The meaning is to shut in or bolt in. It has the idea of shutting the door. When Noah saw that his family was aboard the ark and all the animals were secure, then "the Lord closed it [the door of the ark] behind him" (Gen. 7:16). The ark was sealed for its historic voyage.

But instead of being in an ark, in a place of safety due to one's obedience, Jonah found himself shut in a place of great danger because of his disobedience. The hidden rocks that plunged into the sea were his dungeon walls. The bars, those long submarine reefs of rock, were his prison bars. The seaweeds were his chains. What a vivid description of complete bondage—a helpless prisoner held captive beneath the blue waves!

At the end of verse 6 we have a beam of sunlight that pierces these murky waters. Jonah cries out, "But Thou hast brought up my life from the pit, O Lord my God."

He emphatically repeats that grand title, "O Yahweh my Elohim." Jonah responds in praise to the Lord's deliverance

85

from drowning and from corruption.

How much this should remind us of the helpless situation of Ephesians 2:1-3: dead in sin ... walking according to the standards of this world ... living according to the lusts of our flesh, indulging in carnal desires ... being children of wrath.

But Ephesians 2:4-6 continues, "But God [that's where anything of worth begins], being rich in mercy, because of His great love with which He loved us, even when we were dead ... made us alive together with Christ ... and raised us up with Him, and seated us with Him in the heavenly places in Christ Jesus."

The Old Testament also illumines our understanding of God's character: "He raises the poor from the dust, and lifts the needy from the ash heap" (Ps. 113:7). "He brought me up out of the pit of destruction, out of the miry clay; and He set my feet upon a rock making my footsteps firm" (Ps. 40:2).

Praise our wonderful God that He never leaves us in the helpless condition in which He finds us! From death to life, from poverty to riches, from despair to hope, God's salvaging business is complete!

Lord, I Am Praying!

"While I was fainting away, I remembered the Lord; and my prayer came to Thee, into Thy holy Temple" (2:7). Jonah is reminding God that in this despicable predicament he prayed, he remembered the Lord.

"His soul fainted." His soul collapsed and fell upon itself. Because of the situation he was in, at the brink of blackout and death, Jonah's soul was covered over with a film that clouded his eyes and numbed his brain. It is a word used in the Old Testament to describe an actual fainting because of excessive exhaustion, thirst, or hunger.

Right at the precipice of death, when the vision is foggy and the mind is dizzy, Jonah remembers God. The words mean to recall to mind, to fix on the mind. This kind of remembrance should decidedly affect our actions.

It's the very word used by the crucified thief in Luke 23:42. As he hung next to the body of our dying Saviour, he said,

"Jesus, remember me when You come in Your kingdom!" He had a heart fixed upon Jesus as his only hope. Jesus' gracious response to his plea was, "Truly I say to you, today you shall be with Me in Paradise" (Luke 23:43). From pain to paradise, God remembers our need!

As we celebrate the ordinance of the Lord's Supper, this observance is a corporate remembrance of the death of Jesus Christ (see 1 Cor. 11:24,25). The word is different, but the concept is similar.

Our privilege is to live moment-by-moment with the focus of our minds and hearts in remembrance of God.

Lord, I Am Empty!

As we listen to Jonah praying, wouldn't you say that this is praying in a tight spot? Whenever the pressures mount, our prayers have an amazing way of getting very intense. Have you ever done this before? You've tried everything else, but now that you are between a rock and a hard place, all you can do is pray in faith!

The words in verse 8 are significant: "Those who regard vain idols forsake their faithfulness." This is an important turning point in Jonah's communion with the Lord. He puts his finger on the very crux of the problem.

Jonah now comes to the point of self-evaluation, and he mentions those who regard vain idols. The idea here is that of keeping or paying attention to "empty vanities." The word is used of the watchman of a city who waits, scanning the horizon for danger signals. It is also used of a person keeping the Sabbath or keeping covenant with God. Another use is found in describing the actions of the person in charge of King David's concubine, one keeping his house.

The impact of this phrase is vital to grasp because it contains a very personal element, a very intense involvement with deep concern. Jonah says that those who have this kind of regard for empty idols are the very ones who have trouble with their faith.

From the idea of guarding, keeping, and watching, the Hebrews used a related word to designate one's eyelid. Why?

Since the eyelid guards the precious eye from injury and dust and smoke, it forms a protective shield around a very beautiful organ.

People who pay attention to worthless, empty idols are in for trouble! The writer of Ecclesiastes uses the phrase "vanity of vanities." The theme portrayed in Ecclesiastes is the total emptiness of a life apart from God, where nothing is able to satisfy the inner longings of the human heart. Pascal said that the God-shaped vacuum in the heart of man could only be satisfied by the Creator Himself. John Calvin said that idols are "all inventions with which men deceive themselves."

Let's bring this statement closer to home. Do you catch what Jonah is saying? He is coming to the point where he realizes that he is no different from those unbelieving sailors on board the ship. They had their little gods and idols, but in the midst of the storm they were utterly powerless! The mariners called, but no one answered.

But what was Jonah's idol? After all, he did have a relationship with Yahweh, and not with any foreign idol made of stone or wood. It is here that God very tenderly, yet very convincingly, drives home the point that Jonah's idol was himself! Self was his "empty vanity."

Jonah's idol was not an obvious item to most onlookers. It was that inner self, the sinful nature of his humanity, that he worshiped. He didn't want to listen to God's will because he had his own ideas. Jonah guarded these; he clung to them. He fled from the presence of God because he paid attention to what was important to *him* and not to *what God was telling him.*

Jacques Ellul writes in his book, *The Judgment of Jonah*, that when man stakes his life on the idols of money or of the state, he does not know personal mercy:

> For these idols which help him to love are without mercy. They can solve his problems. They can grant him happiness, power, even virtue and good. But they cannot give him the very thing he needs, mercy. For these idols have no heart. No relation of love can be set up with them, only relations of possession. If the

one loves, the other possesses. The man who loves money or the state is not loved by them; he is owned. This is why so many fundamental problems of man cannot be solved by these powers. For man has definitive need only of one thing, to be loved, which also means to be pardoned and lifted above himself. None of these idols (least of all *eros*, love) can do this for him. But man does not know this, or hear it, until he has learned the emptiness of idols, until he has been disillusioned, until in truth he finds himself naked and without mercy, until he begs in an empty world for the mercy which cannot come to him from the world. To this stripped man God responds as he does to Jonah, and Jonah learns where mercy is to be had, and who can give it to him, and he gets it because for once in his life he turns to the one who is in fact merciful.[2]

What Is My Idol?

Does this strike a familiar note with you? I can think of so many times in my own life when the ideas and desires that I fancied most took precedence over what God was teaching me. I'm ashamed of that. Idols—all kinds of them! We know that when temptation comes knocking at our door, only sin will go to answer!

That's what Jonah is saying. The temptation to regard something really worthless came knocking at his door, and he went immediately to let it in! Then he closed the door and spent time enjoying that idol—guarding it and paying close attention to it. You see, Jonah could not get God's perspective because he was totally immersed in his own selfishness. You cannot serve God while clinging to the idol of self.

What kinds of idols are we tenaciously guarding? To which empty vanity do we still cling? TV is perhaps Public Idol Number One. It is frightening to read the statistics on how much time is consumed in American homes while seated passively in front of the "idiot box"!

And then there is excessive eating, the sports mania, a drive for scholarship or profession, homemaking, hobbies, or any number of other things. The list is endless. Whatever takes up an inordinate amount of time can easily become one of our empty idols.

Some of us men get so wrapped up with athletics and the array of competitive sports that we nearly have a coronary when someone interrupts our viewing of the Dallas Cowboys or the Cincinnati Reds! We know the lifetime statistics of all the players in the National Baseball League, but we're "out to lunch" in knowing the personal needs of our families.

But it's not just the men who are at fault. Some ladies become so proficient at dusting and creating an appealing home museum that they begin to regard their family members as display articles, never really knowing how to relate to them as people!

My counsel to the diligent homemakers is not to drop the cloth or leave the broom, but to seek for a proper balance of your time and priorities. And you sports fans, male or female, don't think this exhortation is anti-athletic—but why not strive to let a game or two slip by so you can spend some needed time with your loved ones?

As I take a personal inventory I see a number of areas that God has had to deal with. During college and my first few years at seminary one of my prize idols was a big library. Books, books, and more books! I wanted to let people see how many I had so that I could be thought of as someone with a lot of savvy upstairs.

And to top it all off I developed a skilled talent in making "idol stands"—bookshelves. Countless hours would be spent in sawing, planing, and staining beautiful pine shelves. Once completed, I would gingerly place my idols on them as the finishing touch.

Somebody would come into my study and say, "Gosh, Devine, you've got quite a library here!"

"Thank you."

"How many of these books have you read?"

That question always left me looking for another topic of discussion! I avoided the truth by simply giving some vague answer. I was more concerned with the status associated with a stack of books than with their educational importance. How I thank God for giving me victory over that kind of attitude! I no longer regard books as idols for display, but I view them with appreciation as tools for my personal development.

The Empty Toys

Empty people collect beautiful "toys." Spend a few moments surveying the cults and the contemporary religious scene. People are building multimillion-dollar structures, temples, and worship facilities with outlandish material luxuries —all in the name of religion. Some of these monstrosities would make our Powellhurst Baptist Church look like a doghouse! I'm so glad that God's eye is not focused on buildings, but on our personal character.

Emptiness cannot be hidden or covered over for any length of time. A life stuffed full of mundane niceties will soon develop indigestion—a few burps, a sigh, and then a first-class stomachache! Toys, idols, anything apart from a satisfying, personal relationship with the Lord Jesus Christ will bring untold misery. Satisfaction comes for a price, already paid in full for us by the Saviour Himself. As John reminds us so aptly, "Little children, guard yourselves from idols" (1 John 5:21).

Do not overlook the frightful conclusion: "[They] forsake their faithfulness." Idol-watchers desert and dismiss faithfulness. This word, *hesed*, literally means mercy, and it is the beautiful designation of God's consistent, loyal, covenant love for His own.

God's loyal love for us is unconditional. This means that we can't earn it and that He never gives up loving us. "God is love" (1 John 4:8,16). His very nature is love-saturated! It never "dries up." His loving resources are infinite, and we can always count on His unending supply.

"Sorry, Lord, I've got to spend time polishing my idols. I don't really need your love right now; my idol keeps me warm!" Actually, the word used here is very strong—"to forsake God Himself." Appealing substitutes—empty, vain

91

idols—rob us of experiencing the very love of God!

The Love of God

Here is an interesting thought. When the Hebrews wanted an appropriate designation for "stork," they used the word for mercy as the basis. In their estimation, the action of the mother stork in tenderly and lovingly caring for her young needed to be captured by a special word. So they chose the very word which signifies the tender love of Yahweh!

That is the very same relationship that God wants to develop with you! He longs to have you experience His tender, consistent, unconditional love.

Intimate fellowship with Jesus Christ will allow the light of His truth (righteous principles and character) to expose our "vain idols." The proper position before God is to have the light of God's Word shine into every area. The light will expose the sin as well as illumine the good works.

The invitation before us is well stated by Paul in 2 Corinthians 5:15: "And He died for all, that they who live should no longer live for themselves, but for Him who died and rose again on their behalf."

EFFECTIVE SERVICE FOR GOD
BEGINS WITH A FULLY SURRENDERED LIFE.

Footnotes

1. See Delitzsch's comments on this in "Jonah," *Minor Prophets* Commentary on the Old Testament, vol. 10 (Grand Rapids: Eerdmans, 1971 reprint), p. 402.
2. Jacques Ellul, *The Judgment of Jonah* (Grand Rapids: Eerdmans, 1971), pp. 57,58.

9 | Whatever Goes Down Must Come Up
Jonah 2:9,10

As we studied the first verses in this section (2:5-8) we observed how God purged Jonah of self. That process is always painful because of our stubborn self-love. We all like to sing the tune, "I love me, I love myself, I even love my picture on the shelf!" The purging of self is a process that we must learn repeatedly.

We might capture the emphasis of 2:5-8 by several phrases: 1) God's final preparation is the resignation of self, and one's restoration to service; 2) God delights in filling an empty vessel; 3) A vessel must be emptied of self before God employs it for service.

Man must come to the place where he realizes his complete *inability* before he can recognize God's complete *ability!* John 15:5 tells us, "I am the vine, you are the branches; he who abides in Me, and I in him, he bears much fruit; for apart from Me you can do nothing." It is only as we recognize this fact that we will be able to do "all things through Him who strengthens me" (Phil. 4:13).

Prepared for Service

There is a striking similarity between verse 9 and the end of chapter 1: "Then the men feared the Lord greatly, and they offered a sacrifice to the Lord and made vows" (1:16). "But I will sacrifice to Thee with the voice of thanksgiving. That which I have vowed I will pay. Salvation is from the Lord" (2:9).

This same concept of sacrifice and vows was first encountered at the point of the Phoenician sailors' conversion, when they offered a sacrifice and made vows to the Lord.

All of verse 9 is filled with words of praise and worship, and Jonah ends his prayer in joyous thanksgiving. The same thought is found in Hebrews 13:15: "Through Him then let us continually offer up a sacrifice of praise to God, that is, the fruit of lips that give thanks to His name."

Filled by Christ
If I were to pick a favorite text in the Bible it would have to be Colossians 2:10: "And in Him you have been made complete, and He is the head over all rule and authority."

When I meditate on the fact that I am complete in Christ, filled to the brim out of His fullness, then my heart leaps to thank God for His wonderful work in my behalf. I am right now a *whole* person—not some sort of zombie, half-dead and half-alive.

Our boy Matthew used to enjoy helping Lynn and me with the dishes after dinner. We would be working and talking at the sink, and Matt would manage to squeeze between us and play with the bowls and cups, splashing around and filling them with water. One time he filled a large mixing bowl full of water and then dumped a small cup into it. The cup was immediately filled with water and gurgled to the bottom of the bowl. Such is Paul's emphasis in Colossians 2:10. We are filled out of Christ's fullness! The song we teach our children tells us the same thing:

>Running over, running over,
>My cup is full and running over.
>Since the Lord saved me
>I'm as happy as can be!
>My cup is full and running over!

We're *completely full* in Him who is our life! This is now Jonah's condition—filled with the precious experience of God's deliverance.

The idea of completeness is seen in the word "sacrifice." According to the Levitical feasts, Israel was to acknowledge God's goodness by participating in a series of offerings. Instead of an animal sacrifice, Jonah willingly offers his sacrifice of praise with the voice of thanksgiving (see Lev. 7:12-15). Jonah gives evidence of being complete in that he is now free to offer praise to God.

Something had really taken place in Jonah! This was no surface movement of the lips, but his heart had truly been mellowed by a sovereign God. Jonah's determined commitment to pay his vow tells of his willingness to fulfill his responsibility. His life had been brought under proper submission to the Lord.

Do What You Promise

In a recent counseling session, a Christian brother shared with me the agony of not living up to this principle of keeping the vows we make.

Carl had moved to Oregon from California. Before he came northward he had amassed several debts with close friends. Some of these outstanding debts were easily forgotten in the excitement of a new job and the readjustments required in another residence.

But Carl's first year in Oregon was utterly miserable. His spiritual walk became a bitter experience of guilt and frustration as he struggled to seek the troubling source of his depression.

Our final session was a jubilant time of praise as he shared the victory of knowing God's will for his life. Carl admitted the fact that he had made several specific financial vows with friends in California. He had consciously tried to push these aside in his attempt to get a "fresh start" in Oregon.

Vows are binding agreements of trust. They must be kept. If they are not, our credibility suffers and we suffer too! Carl saw the truth of this and scheduled a priority list to meet his neglected financial debts. He kept his vows. Liberty within limits has become the exciting experience of his Christian life!

Salvation Is of the Lord

Jonah concludes his prayer with one of the most stupendous statements that could fall from human lips: "Salvation is of Yahweh." In this accolade of praise the humbled prophet gives evidence of a heart truly resigned to the sovereign will of God. The struggle with self is over, and Jonah has been delivered from the plague of pride!

Why is this proclamation so significant? In my earlier days I remember getting extremely irritated at bumper stickers and highway signs proclaiming "Jesus Saves!" and other gospel mottoes. "Why can't these religious fanatics keep their propaganda to themselves?" I used to say. As a violent, unbelieving protester I carried on a personal smear campaign against such advertising practices. But how glad I am to see in retrospect how the lovely Spirit of God turned my bitter attitude into one of joy and praise for the astounding reality that Jesus *does* save—He even saved me!

The word "salvation" carries with it the idea of deliverance. The term describes deliverance from enemies in battle or the fact of being rescued from perils and troubles. The focus begins as something external, but it also has definite implications on the internal aspect of being brought to a place of safety.

The Impact of God's Love

The tremendous impact of the work of Jesus Christ in redeeming men was graphically portrayed to me by my dad. This is the way it happened.

When I was in grade school I fell in love with the game of baseball. Every day would be saturated with time spent at the Longfellow Playground. We had teams from the school, from the neighborhood, from anywhere we could scrape together nine eager ball players! When we weren't playing, the guys were busily trading baseball cards and chewing the big hunks of bubble gum that came with each packet of cards.

I had become acquainted with a new friend who shared the same love as I did. One day Stan invited me to his home to play catch. Excited and carefree, we bundled up our mitts, bats, and baseballs, and headed toward his home, which was located at the other end of town. Unfortunately, I forgot to tell dad where I was going.

Stan and I played together all day long, but I didn't bother to call my parents. Late in the afternoon dad began to get worried when I didn't show up for dinner. He called all over town trying to find his son. He phoned all my friends (all three of them!).

After no contact, he tried something else. Knowing that we had often gone down to the swamp after school to play on the rafts, dad frantically drove down there in hopes of locating his missing son. He ran down the rocky embankment to the water's edge and began calling out for me: "Jimmy, Jimmy!" No answer. He then took off his shoes, rolled up his trousers, and waded out into that black murky mud. He put his hands down into the swampy water, and with tears filling his eyes he continued to call out for his boy. He called out for the one he loved, the one who he thought might have fallen off a raft and been hurt or even drowned.

Later that night, tired and hungry, I came bouncing in. "Hi, dad! How's things?" There was an unmistakable look of delight and relief that came over his face that I'll never forget. He threw his arms around me and told me what he had done.

Here is the picture of our competent Deliverer, the Lord Jesus—the One who waded out into the swamp of human sin and called us home to Himself. He desires our fellowship as His sons.

Do you love Him more each day? Are you conscious of His grace and "the excellencies of Him who has called you out of darkness into His marvelous light" (1 Pet. 2:9)? The psalmist has written, "He raises the poor from the dust, and lifts the needy from the ash heap, to make them sit with princes" (Ps. 113:7,8), and David writes in Psalm 40, "He brought me up out of the pit of destruction, out of the miry clay; and He set my feet upon a rock making my footsteps firm . . . . There is none to compare with Thee" (vv. 2,5).

Bill Gaither's song, "He Touched Me," captures the joy of a rescued heart:[1]

> Shackled by a heavy burden,
> 'Neath the load of guilt and shame;
> Then the hand of Jesus touched me
> And now I am no longer the same!

The Dynamics of Deliverance

Jonah had come to appreciate what we might term the "satisfaction of salvation" or the "dynamics of deliverance." Our salvation is not a dead issue or a static fact. Rather, our salvation has a dynamic quality that should affect our lives on a daily basis.

When the apostle Paul was tied up in knots over his own conflict between the weakness of his flesh and the godly desires of his heart (see Rom. 7:14-25), he began to wage the battle that every child of God goes through. This is no isolated incident that just happens with great spiritual leaders; it is something you face in *your* life!

Paul agonized over this internal battle. He admitted his own wishing (see Rom. 7:18) and yet saw his own wretchedness (see Rom. 7:24). But look how God broke through and gave him the glorious insight he needed! Jesus Christ was his victory; the Lord Jesus Christ was Paul's Deliverer. He had rescued him from the penalty of sin, and now He was also bringing him to the safe assurance that his secure salvation in Christ was a transforming process in which Jesus became more and more the Lord of his life—his true Commander-in-Chief!

Not only has the Lord rescued us from *sin*, but He specializes in delivering us from the *sins* that we continue to commit. That's what a dynamic salvation is all about—God *continues* to mold us into the character of His Son, into godly men and women. The process will be completed when we meet Jesus face-to-face at the time of the rapture of the Church, the body of Christ (see 1 Thess. 4:15-17).

Think of this—until that moment comes, we have an Advocate in the Person of Jesus Christ who is continually cleansing us and presenting our needs before the Father's throne! What a combination!

> A *past* salvation—secure in Christ through the work on the Cross (Regeneration).
>
> A *present* salvation—the ongoing work of the Spirit in the believer's heart to make him more like Jesus (Sanctification).

A *future* salvation—that hopeful expectation of having God's transforming work completed when Jesus takes the Church as His eternal bride! (Glorification and Adoption).

No wonder Paul got excited when he cried out, "Thanks be to God through Jesus Christ our Lord!" (Rom. 7:25). He knew that Jesus was his totally adequate Deliverer.

"Salvation is from the Lord." The very word for "salvation" that Jonah uses is the root from which the name Jesus is derived. The personal name of God's Son was "Jesus" (Luke 1:31). His name is a shortened form of *Yeshoshu'a* or *Yeshu'a*, meaning "Yahweh is help or salvation." It was this one, Jesus, through whom God was to bring salvation (see Matt. 1:21 and Luke 2:25-38).

Lord, You Are My Life

At this point in Jonah's experience an incredible thing happened. The fish got a divine stomachache—Jonah didn't taste too good! So out he came. "Then the Lord commanded the fish, and it vomited Jonah up onto the dry land" (2:10).

Jonah landed (right side up!) on the shore. God returned His servant to the place of his disobedience. That's where we must all begin again. It's not that we should or can correct all the errors of our past, but we need to go back and recognize what went wrong in our walk with the Lord and then admit our transgression, confess it, and begin walking with our Lord in "newness of life" (Rom. 6:4).

Regaining Lost Love

I remember seeing Anthony Quinn in the movie, *The Shoes of the Fisherman.* It was the dramatic story of a faithful man who was elevated from a prison camp to the position of Pope of the Catholic Church. While in the midst of ecclesiastical pressures, the Pope (Quinn) slips off his robes, "escapes" from the Vatican, and goes out into the streets of Rome to mingle with the common people he served. During his unprecedented and unorthodox venture, the Pope meets a despondent woman who had reached the stage of despair in her marriage and is now aimlessly walking the streets. The brief conversation with the disguised Pope made an impression on my heart:

Pope: Tell me, what happened to you?

Woman: My husband—I've lost him; our love is gone—

Pope: What are you going to do?

Woman: I don't know. We've lost it, but I *still* love him—

Pope: Do you know how to find the love you have lost? You must go back, back to that place where you lost it, and recover that precious treasure.

When the glorified Christ sent a message to the church of Ephesus (see Rev. 2:1-7), He specifically called their attention to the fact that "you have left your first love" (v. 4). Though the church had labored tirelessly and had even exposed false apostles, still Jesus exhorted them for having left their first love, the Lord Himself!

His command was threefold: "[1] Remember therefore from where you have fallen, and [2] repent and [3] do the deeds you did at first" (v. 5).

How subtle are Satan's counterfeit tactics! If he can but muddle our thinking or dislodge our devotion from the Lord Jesus, he has won the battle. "Do anything, Christian! Do something even spiritual or religious, but don't focus your heart's desires on Jesus!" The devil knows that as we "look unto Jesus, the author and perfecter of faith" (Heb. 12:2), our personal experience of Christ's victory is strengthened (see also 2 Cor. 2:14).

Perhaps that is just what God had in mind for Jonah. I don't want to read too much into this statement, but I believe that God was returning Jonah to the dry land for another chance, a fresh start, a new opportunity to trust the God who rescued him!

As Jesus Christ was delivered from death's grasp by the power of God (see Rom. 1:4), so Jonah was rescued alive from his watery grave. The symbolism of Christ is completed with this verse. For our Lord it was a real death, burial, and resurrection; for Jonah it was a near drowning, a sloshy ride in a fish, and a free trip back to land. The "type" (picture) foreshadows the reality. As Matthew records Jesus' words, "Something greater than Jonah is here" (Matt. 12:39-42)!

Jonah has now come full circle. After having at first refused the will of God, he now responds to the mercy of God. The conclusion of Jonah chapter 2 can be spelled out with three R's: Rebuked, Restored, and Returned.

This must have been a glorious moment for Jonah, for we see in the beginning of chapter 3 a new man with the vigor and determination of a new convert. God has prepared His man in the quiet recesses of the sea to "stand in the gap" (Ezek. 22:30) and to proclaim the Word of the Lord! Jonah had finally learned that

EFFECTIVE SERVICE FOR GOD
BEGINS WITH A FULLY SURRENDERED LIFE.

Footnote

1. William J. Gaither, "He Touched Me," *When All Else Fails* (Alexandria, Ind.: Gaither Music Co., 1963). Used by permission.

10 | God of the Second Chance
Jonah 3:1–4

The small plane skipped through the night skies as the pilot's voice echoed the storm warnings over the intercom to the passengers who sat silently in the rear. It was eight years ago that I found myself on this midnight ride from Dallas, Texas, to Fort Polk, Louisiana.

As the plane hit the turbulent winds the aircraft was bounced around and shaken like a baby's rattle. Inner fears and anxieties came to the surface of my mind. I had just resigned from Dallas Theological Seminary after nearly a year's stay. The battle of guilt tore at my guts and almost smothered me.

I had left the instruction of the Word of God by some of the finest professors in the land. My young spiritual walk with God had been stretched to growing proportions, but that was all behind me now. Next destination: the receiving station of the United States Army!

Instead of donning a coat and tie, my new wardrobe would be the drab greens of Uncle Sam! Instead of carrying a load of Christian books and language references, I would be trudging through the incredibly hot sun and sand of Louisiana, loaded down with a knapsack and a weapon. Instead of proclaiming "Love! Love!" I would soon be following orders and yelling "Kill! Kill!" as the new trainees practiced for hours with gleaming bayonets protruding from their rifles.

"Culture shock" is what they call it, and I had a first-class case of this disease. At one time I thought this malady pertained only to overseas travel, but I quickly discovered that it can be contracted right in this country!

Can God Use a Dropout?

Had I missed the will of God? Could God still use a drop-out? These questions lingered over my head like a sheet of iron, pressing their weight until I could feel the burden down to my toes. The decision to withdraw from school came at a most crucial time. I felt like a man caught in a whirlpool, being sucked down into the vortex with nothing to grab.

Have you ever labored with the gnawing pangs of guilt that seem to say, "You're finished! You're on the shelf for God. God cannot use a failure"? Perhaps you haven't had the experience of withdrawing from school; maybe your battle with guilt and failure came from another arena of life. But still the force of it all was crushing. An illness, a disappointment, a rash decision, an unkind word—any of these can start the process.

A man who attended our church shared with me an experience that has plagued him for years. Earlier in his life John had sensed that God was leading him into the Christian ministry as a full-time occupation. He realized his need for training at a Bible college, but when it came time to enroll he turned away to a secular job with a local manufacturing firm. Now, even after 20 years, those disturbing thoughts still trouble him. John feels that he really missed the will of God for his life!

This is not an isolated illustration. In counseling with young couples, the thoughts of having married the wrong person frequently stir the waters of dissatisfaction. Frustrated expectations, personality weaknesses, and a constellation of other factors seem to invade the peace between partners. And so one (or both) mates quietly wrestle with these thoughts deep inside, looking through selfish spectacles at how their wife/husband has been such a disappointment.

As we turn to the third chapter of Jonah, the Lord greets us with some of the most comforting words in the entire Bible! *God never discards a forgiven life!* In other words, *true repentance for past sin qualifies us for present service.* This is Jonah's experience as this chapter unfolds. It can be *your* experience too!

103

The Second Word

"Now the word of the Lord came to Jonah the second time" (3:1). This phrase is almost identical to the opening sentence of the book (1:1), but something is altered here. The words "the second time" stand out emphatically.

In 1:1 we were introduced to Jonah, Amittai's son. But by the time we reach Jonah 3:1, we have been thoroughly introduced to this runaway who is now being restored to profitable service. So the Spirit of God eliminates any further introduction, and the narrative moves forward.

Have you ever asked yourself, "How many times can God forgive?" If you have been a good student of the Scriptures you will recall the words of Jesus in Matthew 18:22. Peter had asked the Lord about keeping a tally on forgiving others, and then he proposed an impressive-sounding number—"up to seven times" (Matt. 18:21). I imagine that sounded more than fair to Peter, but not so to the Lord. Jesus responds, "I do not say to you, up to seven times, but up to seventy times seven!" The implication was that Peter should keep on forgiving those who offended him again and again. God's forgiveness is infinite; it has no limit. Our forgiveness should assume this quality as well.

There are no boundary markers on a forgiving heart. Perhaps this is why the Lord Jesus expanded His emphasis on the essential behavior of forgiving others when He was teaching the disciples how to pray: "For if you forgive men for their transgressions, your heavenly Father will also forgive you. But if you do not forgive men, then your Father will not forgive your transgressions" (Matt. 6:14,15; see also Matt. 18:23–35).

No Limit to Love

Men measure spiritually by the yard or the pound, by so long or so much. But God is in the business of smashing such a human perspective of lengths and amounts. The believing child of God has had the love of God poured in his heart through the Holy Spirit (see Rom. 5:5), and this love (*agape*, an expression of care not based on merit or worth) is not to be bottled up in pint-size or quart-size bottles or in five-pound boxes!

Jonah has been forgiven and forged into a new man. He has taken a giant step in trusting God with his life. The fires of affliction have burned off his rough corners, and the balm of God's love and grace has been the healing salve.

So the challenge for Jonah is a challenge for us too. It is not how many times I can disobey God and get away with it, nor how many times I can outsmart my heavenly Father, but how soon I will let the Spirit of God control my life in every area!

God's discipline has now ceased, for Jonah is now ready for service. Hebrews 12 talks about God's divine discipline as a Father toward His own children. The purpose of that discipline, though unpleasant and very painful when we are going through it, is that in the end we will share in the very character and holiness of God (see Heb. 12:10). And there is another thought attached to this. Not only does God take us through a discipline experience so that we can share in His very character, but He also disciplines us so that we can share in His sovereign purposes (see Rom. 8:28). When God is pleased to use us for His glory, this is positive proof that He is at peace with us.

How many people are just waiting for a second chance or a new start, yet are still holding on to that sin that caused them to fail the first time around? So the word comes to Jonah, the very Word of Yahweh, and this time God's man is really listening!

Jonah Listens

"Arise, go to Nineveh the great city and proclaim to it the proclamation which I am going to tell you" (3:2). As the word comes, what does Jonah hear? What does he perceive this second time around, as he receives another opportunity to obey? I imagine that Jonah had settled down by now, and that some time had elapsed since his arrival back to land. We do not know. More than likely he began to settle down and pay the vows he made, and to complete what he had promised before the Lord.

Imagine the personal thrill Jonah experienced as God spoke to him again! It probably stunned him at first. "You mean, Lord, you still want to use me?" The mixture of excitement and humility was perhaps a startling combination.

"Arise, go." It was the same command, the same ministry that Jonah had earlier rejected. When the Lord called Ezekiel He said to the prophet, "And you, son of man, neither fear them nor fear their words, though thistles and thorns are with you and you sit on scorpions; neither fear their words nor be dismayed at their presence, for they are a rebellious house. But you shall speak My words to them whether they listen or not, for they are rebellious" (Ezek. 2:6,7; cf. vv. 1-5).

The authoritative word of the Lord strikes a receptive heart. There is no rebellion here, no hesitancy, no shrinking back with excuses. Jonah did not even ask God how many of his hearers would repent! How this scene differs from the occasion on which the Lord called His servant Moses in Exodus 3 and 4! This Bible hero offered God a grocery list of excuses.

Why Do We Balk?

Why do we balk when the Lord moves our heart in a certain direction? Are we fearful that He will leave us hanging in midair with no direction, no power, no assurance of His presence? Such thoughts that clamor for our attention indicate our nearsighted view of a Father who stands ready and fully able to meet every single need in our walk with Jesus Christ!

Look how Yahweh provided for Jonah. God tells His prophet to proclaim (literally, to "cry out" or "preach") a special message to the Ninevites. Perhaps the dialogue went something like this:

"But, Lord, what can I tell them? I haven't even studied for my message yet! I've just arrived back home from my ocean cruise!"

"Jonah, arise and go. I will provide you with the message you need."

"Lord, you're terrific. I'm ready to go and I'll take your message to that city."

It sounds like a dream come true. The prophet was being sent as an itinerant preacher with a message prepared directly by God Himself! Do you see the point? Was the Lord concerned whether Jonah had prepared a homiletical presentation with three main points and a poem? No! He was concerned to know that Jonah had a *prepared heart!* The task of the preacher or any ministering believer is to first put his heart in order so that the message of God's loving grace will overflow from an honorable vessel (see Rom. 9:21-24).

MacLaren's words are timely: "They [those who bear God's message] should sound it out loudly, plainly, urgently, with earnestness and marks of emotion in their voice. Languid whispers will not wake sleepers. Unless the messenger is manifestly in earnest, the message will fall flat. Not with bated breath, as if ashamed of it; nor with hesitation, as if not quite sure of it; nor with coldness, as if it were of little urgency,—is God's Word to be pealed in men's ears. The more simply he repeats the stern, plain, short message, the more likely it is to impress. God's Word, faithfully set forth, will prove itself."[1]

Now don't get too hasty in moving on to verse 3! Notice how the Lord concludes His conversation with Jonah: "Proclaim to it the proclamation which I am going to tell you." There is a promise here. Jonah is not going to be traveling alone, God is with him. God always operates that way. Jesus said something similar to this when He met His disciples in Galilee: "Lo, I am with you always, even to the end of the age" (Matt. 28:20). And Paul wrote to the Corinthians, "[we may be] persecuted, but not forsaken" (2 Cor. 4:9). Never is the believer left to stand by himself. God is not a deserter. He is, as the writer of Proverbs put it, "a friend who sticks closer than a brother" (Prov. 18:24).

God never sends us as His witnesses
without *encouraging* us;
without *equipping* us;
without *accompanying* us!

The City Waits

Jesus talked about His witnesses in Acts 1:8. Unto the

107

uttermost parts of the earth the message of God's redeeming love through Jesus Christ is to be proclaimed. Jonah was sent as a preaching witness to the great city of Nineveh.

Lynn and I once had an unusual opportunity to be witnesses. During our first year at Western Conservative Baptist Seminary we managed a 26-unit complex of apartments for a large investment company in Portland. It turned out that one of our tenants was stretching the rules and had brought in a cat without the proper permission.

The cat was a beloved pet, but to the neighboring tenants it soon became a pest! When the couple went on a vacation for several days the cat was left alone in the apartment.

We notified the owners of the building and received authorization to enter the apartment, remove the cat, and take it to the Oregon Humane Society. We followed our instructions.

During my absence the owners of the cat suddenly returned from their trip and immediately hit the panic button over their missing animal. They came stomping over to our place and proceeded to address Lynn in the most vile language possible. The racket was heard in every unit! We explained what we had done and where they could retrieve their pet. Threatening accusations were made as they bolted off in disgust.

Summons to appear in the Multnomah County Small Claims Court arrived a few days later. When the judge asked us to speak as witnesses in behalf of the apartment management, he instructed us to tell him exactly what we saw, heard, and did. He allowed us to discuss only those three areas.

That is what a witness is—someone who faithfully tells what he has seen and heard and done. Jonah was God's human witness, a messenger sent with a timely message of mercy—and time was running out for Nineveh!

In verse 3 we are again reminded that "Nineveh was an exceedingly great city, a three days' walk"! (You will find a map of Nineveh on page 109.) In the Old Testament, when the word "great" is used it is employed in several ways. First, it can be a term describing the magnitude of majesty or glory, as when it is associated with God Himself *(Elohim)*. Second, there is another sense in which the word "great" can denote the magnitude and severity of judgment. We know from the historical records and from archaeology that Nineveh was indeed a large urban center with palaces, show halls, great sculptured art, and a splendid library complex. Though Nineveh was great in size, it was equally great in sin, and the magnitude of God's judgment was soon to be felt by the city's nearly 600,000 inhabitants.

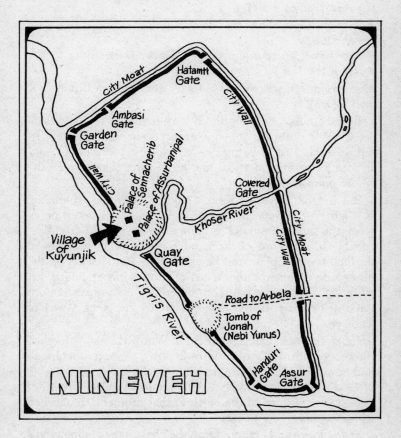

Diagram 3

The phrase "a three days' walk" has been the focus of some attention. The expression has an oriental background and means that it would take an average tourist three days to wander around the city and visit the principal sites of interest.

God never discards a forgiven life; true repentance for past sin qualifies us for present service. Are you beginning to see this tremendous concept? The word of the Lord comes a second time; God's servant listens, and a city waits. The scene is set for verses 3 and 4.

Jonah Obeys

"So Jonah arose and went to Nineveh according to the word of the Lord."

"Now Nineveh was an exceedingly great city, a three days' walk" (3:3).

If you are like me, you find it very tempting to complicate the Christian life. We get so wrapped up in making a "Christians-do-this" list or living by some spiritual formula or constructing elaborate methods and procedures that we miss the whole point altogether.

But Jonah "arose and went." No hesitation, no grumbling, no flight in the opposite direction, no back talk about being given the same command as before. Jonah obeyed God "according to the word of the Lord." The prophet had passed through the discipline and he came out a new person on the other side. And now the Word of God is his standard, his authority. No longer is he torn by selfishness or his stubborn self-will or his patriotic desires, but by the very Word of Yahweh.

Jonah had seen the power of that Word. He had witnessed the grace and mercy of God in his own desperation. Jonah had now become, in short, a walking, talking, living example of God's grace. Frankly, he had more to say than any other man on the surface of the earth at that moment! Jonah had truly met God face-to-face.

When Lynn and I entered into the challenge of being God's servants at Powellhurst Baptist Church, we prayed together for some statement that would define our hearts' desires for that family of believers. The Lord very clearly answered our prayers, and we have since printed that declaration on our stationery and shared it with the body as a personal goal for our church. At Powellhurst we are "Learning Together to Live by the Word of God." All of our thoughts, our activities, and our personal sharing together are directed to be in accordance with the Word of the Lord.

Do we blow it? Are there times of tension and problems? Yes. It would be foolish to say that we've arrived at some pure state of "body life"; we are just beginning! The Word of God, the Bible, is our sole and final authority in all matters of faith and practice. Instead of being some heavenly "answer book" to support our selfish desires, it is God's standard for our lives in helping us understand His Person and program.

I can just see Jonah! He must have been so elated that he had trouble containing his personal joy. The chorus of a popular hymn reads, "Trust and obey, for there's no other way to be happy in Jesus but to trust and obey." We are to be all that God has made us and to enjoy Him in simple, faithful obedience.

The Short Sermon

Someone has given Jonah the title of "First Apostle to the Gentiles." The message that he carried to the violent people of Nineveh was short and to the point. "Then Jonah began to go through the city one day's walk; and he cried out and said, 'Yet forty days and Nineveh will be overthrown' " (3:4). Though composed of only five Hebrew words, the message was tailor-made by God to penetrate the hearts of the people.

Short sermons are not at all a rarity in the Bible. Belshazzar (in the book of Daniel) saw handwriting on the wall that consisted of only four words, yet the impact was clear and convincing! John the Baptist's message was short too: "Repent, for the kingdom of heaven is at hand" (Matt. 3:2). These words are nearly the same as those proclaimed by Jesus Himself in Mark 1:15. The importance of God's message to men is not in the *length* but in the *truth of the words spoken.*

111

Simplicity is always impressive. We have a God who could easily fill the universe with words and string together message upon message without end. But our Lord does not have to be long-winded to get through to us. In fact, in the book of Hebrews, after God had communicated to men through the prophets and in many other ways, the Lord reveals His final word. His ultimate revelation, His supreme sermon, came not in the form of a written manuscript but in the Person of His beloved Son, Jesus Christ (Heb. 1:1-4). The thrust of Jonah's proclamation was not in the weight of his words, but in the fact that he came with the very words God gave him.

Unadorned Power

One of the college girls who had attended a Campus Crusade for Christ training conference in personal evangelism shared an amazing story. Julie related a witnessing experience she had just had on the beaches in California. Part of the training included some live "field" experience, and as she stepped out in faith, Julie's knees were knocking together in fear with every step she took. Timidly she began praying for an opportunity to share Jesus with someone who would want to know about God personally. Soon Julie encountered another girl sitting near one of the docks and engaged her in conversation. When the discussion turned toward spiritual things, she took out a "Four Spiritual Laws" booklet and began stumbling through a gospel presentation.

As Julie told us the story, all she could remember was how miserable she felt: She dropped the booklet into the sand, she missed a few points, and she could hardly manage to hold her friend's attention. When Julie came to a bumbling and embarrassing halt on the final page, she felt certain there would be no further interest. She managed to ask, somewhat dejectedly, "You wouldn't want to receive Jesus Christ as your personal Saviour, would you?"

The girl, who had been listening with no apparent concern, slowly raised her head, only to reveal the tears that gently flowed down her tanned cheeks. She looked Julie right in the eye and said, "Would I? When you were talking a few moments ago I knew this is what I had been searching for. I asked Christ to come into my heart 10 minutes ago!" They sat there together for a moment in quiet reverence and then hugged one another with hearts filled with praise and joy.

What happened? Is the key to our personal evangelism some scintillating presentation of Christ through a flawless delivery? Is it the fact that we have all our theology absolutely down pat? I imagine that Julie's presentation won't go down in the ecclesiastical archives as one of the world's great sermons, but the Spirit of God used her as an ambassador for the Lord Jesus (see 2 Cor. 5:20). As Alexander MacLaren has stated in a message, "Preach, if you like, in the technical sense: have meetings, I suppose, necessarily; but the personal contact is the thing, the familiar talk, the simple exhibition of a loving Christian heart, and the unconventional proclamations in free conversation of the broad message of the love of God in Jesus Christ."[2]

Immediate Obedience

I want you to notice that Jonah went right to the task: "one day's walk." The text gives evidence of the fact that the prophet began immediately to proclaim God's Word. He did not wait for a committee meeting or a decision from the higher-ups. He had a command from God and was walking faithfully in obedience.

"Yet forty days and Nineveh will be overthrown!" The warning was unconditional. The word literally means "to turn upside down from the foundations; to ruin; to devastate." This very expression was used in reference to Sodom and Gomorrah as the Lord moved in on those cities. Great cities are easily overthrown when a great God renders divine judgment!

Notice what Jonah was repeating. Our English translation contains eight words, and the most significant term is one of the shortest. In fact it is the very first word, "yet." "*Yet* forty days." Without that word the message seems to come as a cold and heartless threat. But David reminds us of the Lord's character in Psalm 103:11: "For high as the heavens are above the earth, so great is His lovingkindness toward those who fear Him." "Yet" gives us a hint of God's merciful heart toward this rebellious and sinful city.

The 40-day period was a span of time that was to elapse before destruction fell. But why speak about an interval of time at all? Why didn't God just demolish the city on the spot? He could easily have done this, for the people certainly deserved judgment.

"Yet forty days." The message was clear. God gave them forewarning because His purposes are far holier than ours. *We* see a wrong and leap to punish. *God* sees sin and waits for repentance. The Lord wanted the people for Himself, and repentance takes time!

I don't know how much time today's society has to turn to God in repentance, but I hope that, as we share the message of Jesus Christ with others, the greatest word in our delivery will be the same as Jonah's—"yet." Paul outlined the truth of our witness in Romans 5:8: "But God demonstrates His own love toward us, in that while we were *yet* sinners, Christ died for us."

I've heard some people say that none of us has more than one chance in this life, and that if we blow it, we've had it. But this is man's thinking, not God's. My Bible does not portray the Father as some bitter old man with a black club just waiting to clobber us when we step out of line.

Yes, I do recognize the sobriety of Genesis 6:3 ("My Spirit shall not strive with man forever"), but the context indicated an extreme and willful denial of all godliness and truth, in which "the Lord saw that the wickedness of man was great on the earth, and that every intent of the thoughts of his heart was only evil continually" (Gen. 6:5).

Mercy Toward Manasseh

But has God ever given anyone else a second chance? Yes, He has! Open your Bible to the book of 2 Chronicles. In chapter 33 we read about one of the longest reigns of any king in Judah—55 years! And who do you suppose got this coveted honor? Some choice servant of the Lord? No. In fact, the tragedy of the whole account is that the man who occupied the throne was "Public Nuisance Number One," Manasseh. This fellow started to reign at 12 years of age (compare 2 Kings 21:1-8 for more insight on this evil character) and continued to get worse and worse. Just take a look at his performance record:

- did evil in the sight of the Lord
- rebuilt the high places
- erected altars to the Baals
- worshiped all the host of heaven
- made his sons pass through fire
- practiced witchcraft
- used divination
- practiced sorcery
- dealt with mediums and spiritists
- put idols into the very temple of God!

Here was a man who enjoyed sin and practiced evil to the hilt! Finally, Manasseh was captured with hooks through his nose and was bound with bronze chains and led as a common captive to Babylon.

If there was anyone who did not deserve another chance, it was certainly Manasseh! But God has an incredible ability to get our attention even if we keep on refusing to obey. Second Chronicles 33:12,13 describes an amazing transformation. It's almost beyond imagination, but it actually happened.

Hooked, bound, and captured, Manesseh turns to the Lord in a heartrending act of true repentance. What a loving Father! Verse 13 tells us that, after all Manasseh had done in misleading Judah and causing the people to act more wickedly than Israel's enemies, God "was moved by his entreaty and heard his supplication, and brought him again to Jerusalem to his kingdom. Then Manasseh knew that the Lord was God." The next few verses (2 Chron. 33:14-20) describe Manasseh's great restoration projects, in which he "ordered Judah to serve the Lord God of Israel" (v. 16).

Jonah, Manasseh, Paul, Moses—the list goes on. God does respond to true repentance for past sin, and by His grace He uses such people for His glory. Before going on to the next chapter, do three things right now:

1. *Thank God for His forgiveness.* The fact that God has cleansed your life from the penalty and power of sin is not just a theological nicety, but a dynamic, living reality of grace! Praise Him often for His liberating gift of freeing you from being a slave to sin (Rom. 6:15-22).

2. *By faith, claim the Lordship of Jesus Christ.* This comes in stages as you grow in grace and in the knowledge of Christ. If you are aware of an area in your life where Jesus is *not* Lord, then yield that control to Him. "Lord, I give you the control of my eyes and my thoughts. Lead me away from that which will corrupt my mind and cause me to lust and covet." "Lord, I yield the area of my homemaking to you. Help me to be a Christian woman filled with the joy of the Lord as I vacuum, dust, and wash the clothes."

3. *Trust God to make His will known to you.* God directs your life as you "walk in the light" (1 John 1:7). Don't sit and stew in your guilt, for this will only petrify your spiritual walk before God. (Turn to Appendix and read "How to Know the Will of God.")

The magnificent truth about our heavenly Father is that

GOD NEVER DISCARDS A FORGIVEN LIFE.

Footnotes

1. Alexander MacLaren, *Expositions of Holy Scripture*, vol. 6 (Grand Rapids: Eerdmans, 1942), p. 191.
2. MacLaren, *Expositions of Holy Scripture*, vol. 3, p. 353.

11 | The Greatest Altar Call of All Time
Jonah 3:5–10

The Lord Jesus made a great impression on the gathering crowds as He said, "This generation is a wicked generation; it seeks for a sign, and yet no sign shall be given to it but the sign of Jonah. For just as Jonah became a sign to the Ninevites, so shall the Son of Man be to this generation . . . . The men of Nineveh shall stand up with this generation at the judgment and condemn it, because they repented at the preaching of Jonah" (Luke 11:29,30,32).

We are coming to a fantastic portion of Jonah's drama. In these six concluding verses of chapter 3 we encounter the repentance of the people, the repentance of the king of Nineveh, and even the repentance of God Himself! The truth that develops from this section is that *a godly change of mind will produce a godly character of life.*

The People Repent

"Then the people of Nineveh believed in God; and they called a fast and put on sackcloth from the greatest to the least of them" (3:5).

Jonah's message was only five words long (in Hebrew): "Yet forty days and Nineveh—overthrown!" In man's estimation the scene was ludicrous. Here was a puny man with a puny message who had walked into a gigantic metropolis. Yet, according to God's viewpoint, behind that "puny" man and that "puny" message was the unlimited power of the eternal God! The person who dares to trust God for great

117

things does not need a lengthy theological dissertation to share the riches of God's love and mercy.

Andrew said to his brother, "We have found the Messiah," and Peter believed. All that Philip said to Nathanael (Bartholomew) was a brief word of testimony of how the Scriptures verified Jesus' credentials as Messiah, and to "come and see" (John 1:45,46), and the "man who sat in the shade" became one of Christ's 12 apostles. Some of the shortest messages have produced the greatest results. If we were to condense the appeal of the gospel into one word it would be "come." Yes, God calls us to come: "Come to Me, all who are weary and heavy laden, and I will give you rest" (Matt. 11: 28).

How do we explain such a spontaneous response to Jonah's message? Some have referred to the prophet's strange mannerisms as a Jewish foreigner in Gentile territory. Others have remarked about the physical effects of being in the belly of the fish; those gastric juices could have turned the color of Jonah's skin to a shade of purple, and think what an impact this might have had on the unsuspecting residents of Nineveh! "Hey, here comes the Purple Fish Man!"

Historians tell us that several epidemics had swept through the Nineveh area, taking many lives, and on June 15, 763 B.C., a total eclipse of the sun occurred, which could have sparked many fears and added greatly to the proper climate for this remarkable repentance.[1] Whether these reasons are valid or not, the truth remains that God was moving mightily through the proclamation of His Word. He had sovereignly prepared the heart of His servant and the hearts of the people.

A Change in Devotion

Both the message and the messenger were in harmony with the will of God, and "the people of Nineveh believed in God." There was a change in their devotion. Up to this time the statement in Judges 17:6 could well have applied to the Ninevites, even as it had marked the children of Israel: "Every man did what was right in his own eyes."

The capital of the Assyrian Empire had known lavish luxury, lust, and sensuality of every variety. Here was a city for "swingers," and the people had swung clear out of sight for any human reform! But God saw their desperate need, and the word of the Lord cut into this moral morass like a two-edged sword (see Heb. 4:12). As it pierced into the emptiness of their lives, the Spirit of God changed their devotion to Elohim, the Creator God.

Notice the first words in verse 5: "Then the people." The Ninevites heard the word and heeded the warning; they believed in Elohim. The term for "believe" is interesting. The original idea comes from a word meaning "to support, to undergird, to confirm, to establish." It was used to describe the pillars of a building or a firm resolution. In this case the Ninevites stood firm, for once in their lives, upon the foundation of truth. They stood established upon their Creator.

A Change in Life-style

Not only did the people believe from the heart in this act of repentance, but they also put that belief to work. Their behavior began to change as well: "And they called a fast."

We are told by historians that when ancient peoples called a fast it involved total abstinence from all food until the evening hours. Fasting was not a light matter; it called for some internal fortitude to stick to such a rigid restriction. Something was really happening inside. Behavior was being affected by belief!

A Change in Dress

"[They] put on sackcloth from the greatest to the least of them." Sackcloth was certainly not the latest fashion material from Paris, but a very rough, irritating garment. We would probably get some idea of this if we were to wear a leisure suit made of burlap. A sackcloth "wardrobe" was usually worn to mourn over the dead or display humility. Here was an environment that changed from riches to rags!

Everyone, from the most prominent person to the least important, clothed himself with sackcloth. There was no degree of competition here! All the people, the "great ones" and

119

the "small ones," were leveled by the convicting work of truth. They saw themselves being measured by a holy standard, and they knew that their status in Nineveh would have little effect in diverting God's judgment.

Some amazing things happen when God begins to get hold of a people—not just the king or the executives, but the common people like you and me! The spontaneous power of God through His Word will bring about the greatest revival of all time! *A godly change of mind will lead to a godly character of life.*

The Humbled King

The king of Nineveh must have been sensitive to what was happening in the city, for the news soon reached his ears. "When the word reached the king of Nineveh, he arose from his throne, laid aside his robe from [upon] him, covered himself with sackcloth, and sat on the ashes" (3:6).

"The word" that the king heard was the whole accounting of the uproar and the ministry of the prophet Jonah. Exactly how extensive the report was we do not know. Perhaps the king received a summary of Jonah's background and learned of the prophet's deliverance from the great fish and how the grace of God had preserved him alive from certain death. Perhaps he was informed about Jonah's disobedience and his flight from Yahweh and how God had transformed him. Whatever the exact details were, we can be sure that the king's counselors and intelligence service did their best to make it as thorough as possible.

We are not given the name of the king. Pusey says that since the mission of Jonah occurred toward the end of his prophetic ministry (perhaps during the latter part of Jeroboam's reign), the Assyrian leader in Nineveh was probably Ivalush III, the Pul of Scripture. "For Pul was the first Assyrian monarch through whom Israel was weakened; and God had foreshown by Amos that through the third it would be destroyed."[2]

What did this ruling sovereign do? The proclamation of the word of the Lord took him right out of his throne! He arose, laid aside his regal robe, and joined the people in covering himself with sackcloth. His new "throne" became an ash heap (see Job 1)!

The King's Promotion

The scene must have been electrifying! Here was the king himself, humbled by the message of Jonah and sitting on a pile of dirt with the rough garments of a common mourner!

The king stepped down from his throne, his place of rulership and authority. He stepped down from trusting in his position, and placed his trust in Jonah's God instead. Men would see this act as a demotion, but God viewed it as a promotion. The king also exchanged the robes of royalty for the sackcloth of humility and repentance.

Royal Proclamation

Let's notice the king's proclamation in verses 7 and 8: "And he issued a proclamation and it said, 'In Nineveh by the decree of the king and his nobles: Do not let man, beast, herd, or flock taste a thing. Do not let them eat or drink water. Both man and beast must be covered with sackcloth; and let men call on God earnestly that each may turn from his wicked way and from the violence which is in his hands.' "

The monarch used a Syrian word for decree, and Jonah recorded this word in the original Syrian language. The inclusion of this term gives us further evidence that Jonah was an actual eyewitness to the events that transpired. The decree was made in conjunction with the king's nobles and contained several specific requirements.

"Let neither man nor beast, herd or flock, taste a thing. Do not let them eat or drink water." The king imposed a city-wide fast that even included the animals. This seems rather strange to us, but it was customary at that time to recognize a psychological relationship between a man and his animals. Every man's property and possessions, his herds and his flock, all came under the proclamation of the king. Everyone went on a strict diet!

Perhaps there is a word of application here. What we eat or drink can be as much of a testimony to others as what we verbally express. Paul reminds us, "Whether, then, you eat or drink or whatever you do, do *all* to the glory of God" (1 Cor. 10:31). ·

Christian Extremists

Christians seem to be found either at one end of the scale or the other—either at overindulgence or excessive denial. While Lynn and I were touring the nation's capital, we returned to our hotel for a brief rest before going out for dinner. In the lobby we met some very good friends whom we had known in the army.

In the midst of our conversation together Mike said, "Hey, why don't we let the girls do some shopping so you and I can go have a drink together?" I'll never forget my response. Turning directly toward my friend I answered in a very proud tone, "Oh, *I* don't drink. *I'm* a Christian!"

Lynn was terribly embarrassed and managed to pull me off to the side for a private conference. "Okay, Mr. 'Robert Righteous,' who got the glory with *that* answer, you or God?" That pointed rebuke was just what I needed. I was so proud of what I *didn't* do that my whole attitude was boastful and negative.

Before you come to the conclusion that I am advocating a liberal stand toward alcohol or tobacco, I want you to get the point of this application.

Far too often God's people have no idea *why* they do or don't do certain things. Someone tells us, "If you take a drink you're going to hell!" Or, "If you smoke a cigarette you're out of the kingdom!"

But the real question is, do we know *why* we do the things we do? Have we carefully examined our behavior in every realm and asked ourselves, "Does this glorify the Lord?" The same concept that Paul expresses to the Corinthians is also found in his letter to the Colossians (3:17,23).

When I take an honest, personal inventory of my own

habits, I find that this area of glorifying God in my body is one of my great weaknesses. I'm a snacker! Since Lynn is such an outstanding cook, I have developed my snacking abilities to the point of perfection. From any spot in the house I can catch the aroma of a fresh batch of chocolate chip cookies. And I don't just quit after two or three, but every time I pass the cookie jar my hand reaches in for a few more! The Holy Spirit's control is quenched; I snack, not because I'm doing it to the glory of God, but simply because it is a good-tasting habit.

Oh, the subtlety of our sins! We feel quite safe when it comes to denouncing the sluggard, or the drunk, or those who persist in immorality. But being 10 to 15 pounds overweight is nothing to brag about either! So, fellow snackers, maybe it's time we climb down from our high horses and reexamine what we do, to see if our Lord is being honored by our actions!

The Sackcloth Society

The king of Nineveh's proclamation demanded that "both man and beast must be covered with sackcloth." His decree made sackcloth the "in" style!

The fact that the animals were included along with the people is not too unusual, even in our time. Perhaps you have seen a funeral procession of a noted dignitary, in which the casket was positioned on a horse-drawn wagon. Often the horses themselves have black velvet garments draped over their backs.

Does it matter how we dress? Back to that scale of extremes again. Some Christians spend great sums of money on elaborate clothing in order to keep right in style. Others wear expensive clothing to hide their inner poverty.

And then there are those who choose to wear what I term the "beggar look." This style consists of clothing that is outdated, ill-fitting, and in poor taste. The attempt, mostly unconscious, is to evoke a "poverty-spirituality" response. This mentality is certainly not taught in the Bible, but many believers still insist on appearing in the most outlandish costumes that you could set your eyes upon!

In the spectrum of proper dress we need to point out two brief principles:

1. *Wear clothing that is appropriate for the occasion.* My Christian brother, Greg Rowe, works in a variety of places (mostly industrial) as a testing radiographer. I wouldn't expect him to wear a suit to work just to have a Christian testimony. That would only serve to ruin the suit and draw attention to himself.

Our clothes should evidence proper care and cleanliness. A dirty, unpressed shirt never impressed anyone. The "natural look" seems to be fashionable these days, but let's not make it the nauseating look!

2. *Wear clothing that is appropriate for your age and the times.* One of the most hilarious scenes in our neighborhood was the daily appearance of an older woman, probably about 75, who came prancing down the block in her plaid miniskirt. To make the occasion even more hysterical, she wore bright red rouge on her cheeks that could have been peeled off in layers, and she had a ratted-up hairdo that could have served quite nicely for a bird's nest!

Ridiculous? Not when you consider that there are many Christians who have not graciously accepted their age (younger or older), and who try to dress like some other generation.

"For God sees not as man sees, for man looks at the outward appearance, but the Lord looks at the heart" (1 Sam. 16:7). This is certainly a well-known verse and treasure of insight, but most would take this passage and use it as a proof test for wearing anything they happen to put on.

God does indeed look upon the heart. He knows the true condition of the inner man, whether dressed in silk or sackcloth. But man looks on the outward appearance. *Both* truths are to be noted!

If we were to evaluate the abundant life in Christ according to the outward appearance of some believers, the conclusion would be sad indeed. Perhaps we should be more sensitive to this strategic area of testimony, dressing appropriately to the occasion and to our age and style of the day.

Call to Repentance

"And let men call on God earnestly" (3:8; c.f. Gen. 4:26). The king's order was to cry out to God in earnest prayer. Repentance generally implies a change of attitude and action. There was also to be a change of mind in relation to the people's communication with God. When the Lord changes our heart attitude, there is a transformation in the frequency and intensity of our prayers.

"That each [man] may turn from his wicked way" (3:8). This is what had come up before the Lord. "For their wickedness has come up before Me"(1:2). It was the very character of the Ninevite life-style to be violently wicked.

God's Word demanded repentance. The king's edict was unalterable; all must turn from their wicked life-style. The people were to literally make a turnabout—a decided shift in direction from a style of life that reflected self and sin to one that evidenced the grace of God.

"[Turn] from the violence which is in his hands" (3:8). The idiom used in this phrase is figurative. The people were to turn from the violence of their hands, where their hands had been bent to commit acts of violence. That's the word used here—"palms." Not only does the word point very graphically to a wicked life-style that characterized their lives, but it also marked those specific, personal acts of violence committed with their own hands. The people were to turn from a deeply ingrained style of life. Without the power of God such a requirement would be impossible. But God was working and the people were responding! These were the stipulations of the king's proclamation.

The Appeasement Concept

The king of Nineveh was steeped in the tradition of appeasement. That is, he probably worshiped many gods who sought a particular performance standard in order to be satisfied. Many believers still labor under this concept. Even Paul was quick to exhort the Christians in his letter to the Galatians: "You foolish Galatians, who has bewitched you. . . . are you so foolish? Having begun by the Spirit, are you now being perfected by the flesh?" (Gal. 3:1,3). Even the fleshly efforts of regenerated men are in utter contradiction to the standard of the life of Christ. Diagram 4 illustrates the tension between what *man* says and what *God* declared.

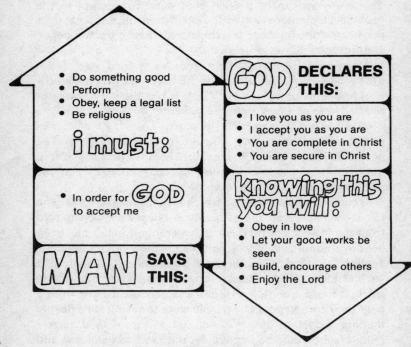

Diagram 4

The performance system that man has designed is a *legal* viewpoint; the second alternative is that of a *gracious* God, the way founded on God's holy character and manifested in His forgiving love. A greater explanation is given by Counts and Narramore in *Guilt and Freedom.*[3]

Note how the king reasons: "Who knows, God may turn and relent, and withdraw His burning anger so that we shall not perish?" (3:9). The king was a religious leader, and the principle of appeasement was foremost in his thinking. The burning, inflamed anger of Yahweh was certainly a real threat to him and to his city.[4] The message of Jonah had gripped his heart!

The word for relent ("repent" in *KJV*) comes from a Hebraic expression meaning "to draw a deep breath" and was used for the panting of horses. Perhaps the connotation symbolized the expression of a deep-seated feeling or emotion. In later usage the word indicated the idea of comfort and compassion.

To translate this phrase into common street language, the king wanted the people to be sure to perform these acts of appeasement so that perhaps God would "take a breather" regarding His divine sentence of doom for Nineveh.

The Repentance of God

Why did God repent? Was it because the people were fasting and wearing the rough sackcloth garments? Was it the unprecedented demotion of the king himself in stepping down from his regal position? No. These were but the outward evidences of an inward transformation.

The text reads, "When God saw their deeds, that they turned from their wicked way, then God relented concerning the calamity which He had declared He would bring upon them" (3:10). The actions of the Ninevites stemmed from a changed heart response. *A godly change of mind will produce a godly character of life.*

Right in the city of Nineveh a revival movement was in full momentum! The people turned, and God saw their hearts. There was real repentance and faith, for God's Word had done its work. God saw people doing things that were totally foreign to their natural desires; He saw them change before His eyes!

And how did God respond? We should emphasize His response in terms of what He did *not* do! The text says He "relented concerning the calamity . . . . And he did *not* do it" (italics added).

There has been far too much confusion concerning this verse. Without probing too deeply into theology, let's examine God's response. We are witnessing the actions of a holy God whose will and purposes are not frivolous, as some would suppose. God does not act in whims, but is perfectly consistent in the execution of His divine decree. His viewpoint is from eternity past to eternity future. He sees the ending from the beginning (see Isa. 46:8-11).

Saul was rejected from being the king of Israel because he had "rejected the word of the Lord" (1 Sam. 15:23). Then the prophet Samuel said to God, "And also the Glory of Israel will not lie or change His mind; for He is not a man that He should change His mind" (v. 29).

It appears from man's finite perspective that God indeed changed His mind. But from the viewpoint of God, the people were being obedient to His command. Remember the words? "Yet forty days and Nineveh shall be overthrown!" It was as if the people could do nothing to avert the impending catastrophe.

But something *did* happen! The people turned in obedience to God's mercy and there was a change in their minds, wills, and emotions. They repented completely; they met God's requirements of mercy. Samuel again unveils the truth: "And Samuel said, 'Has the Lord as much delight in burnt offerings and sacrifices as in obeying the voice of the Lord? Behold, to obey is better than sacrifice, and to heed than the fat of rams'" (1 Sam. 15:22).

No Low Standards

God did not lower His righteous standards. There was no change in His perfect will, nor was there a change in His holy character or the essence of His Being. If Yahweh had "fudged," He would have become less than God. There was no mental switching of gears. The only aspect that changed was the *manifestation* (the outworking) of His will. *We* see "change"; *God* sees the fulfillment of His plan in the very manner He intended it to happen! The writer of Hebrews expresses it this way: "In the same way God, desiring even more to show to the heirs of the promise the unchangeableness of His purpose, interposed with an oath, in order that by two unchangeable things, in which it is impossible for God to lie, we may have strong encouragement, we who have fled for refuge in laying hold of the hope set before us" (Heb. 6:17,18); and again in chapter 13, "Jesus Christ is the same yesterday and today, yes and forever" (Heb. 13:8).

Here is one of the greatest "altar calls" of all time! History has never again witnessed an occurrence of this magnitude in one local area. The sprawling conglomerate of nearly 600,000 in number, were repudiating their wicked ways and turning to God. This dramatic change was in glorious contrast to the unchanging character of God Himself!

Did God know that the people would react in this way? Yes, He did. Did Jonah realize that his simple message would revitalize the city? Perhaps not. He was just being obedient to the "word of the Lord." Peter reminds us of the Lord's desire: "The Lord is not slow about His promise, as some count slowness, but is patient toward you, not wishing for any to perish but for all to come to repentance" (2 Pet. 3:9).

A godly change of mind will produce a godly character of life. God's desire was for the Ninevites to turn to Him in repentance and faith. Paul expressed this same idea in writing to pastor Timothy at Ephesus: "[God] desires all men to be saved and to come to the knowledge of the truth" (1 Tim. 2:4). The exhortation to the believers at Ephesus was to be a praying group led by spiritual men (see 1 Tim. 2:8) and godly women adorned with a quiet attitude that manifested itself in good works (see also 1 Tim. 3; 1 Pet. 3:1-7; Eph. 2:10; 2 Tim. 3:16,17).

Accountable to God

How does this challenge us? When we realize we are no better than the Ninevites, we are ready to face the fact that we are accountable to God, that our life is responsible to the God who created us.

"But how do I turn to Someone I can't see?" The attitude of my heart is what counts, for "God looks upon the heart." He sees me in my sin, for I am morally accountable to Him. The good news of the gospel is that our holy God has provided a Redeemer to break the barrier between Himself and me!

Have you ever written an I.O.U. note? In one sense that is what stood between you and God. But the Bible declares that Jesus Christ has ripped up your I.O.U. note to God and has canceled your moral debt in Christ's death on the cross (see Col. 2:14). Adequate provision for your sin (see Eph. 2:1-3) and separation (see Eph. 2:12) has been taken care of by Jesus. The Son of God stands as the life-link between you and your Creator.

You Must Receive

You have one final obligation. You *must receive* what God has already accomplished in your behalf! A thirsty man can look at a cold glass of water for hours. He can even dip his finger into the glass and feel its wetness. *But he must drink that water* in order for his thirst to be satisfied.

Perhaps you have been an outstanding person who has given himself to others in acts of kindness and love. Maybe you have even been involved in the activities of a local church as an officer. But right now you are terribly aware of the nagging spiritual thirst of your own life. Before reading another page, turn to God in the privacy of your heart and ask Him to forgive you and receive His free gift of life in Jesus Christ.

The Bible declares that "there is salvation in no one else; for there is no other name under heaven that has been given among men, by which we must be saved" (Acts 4:12). Now turn to chapter 10 of Paul's letter to the Romans and read verses 8 to 13. Receive God's grace and invite Jesus to come into your life today (see John 1:12; 2 Cor. 6:2; Rev. 3:20)!

Once you have made this personal decision of trust, turn to the apostle John's first letter near the end of the New Testament. Read 1 John 5:10-15. Spend time meditating on this section and then begin reading the Gospel of Mark. Mark's short, concise style of on-the-spot reporting will give you a fine introduction into the life of Jesus Christ. Decide now to make the reading of God's Word a daily part of your life schedule. May God enrich your life as you learn how to trust

Him more completely and to "grow in the grace and knowledge of our Lord and Savior Jesus Christ" (2 Pet. 3:18).

For you who have already begun this exciting walk with Christ there is abundant application as well! How many areas in your life are still not under the control of the Spirit? Aren't you sick and tired of the constant battle and frustration this is causing in your personal growth? Isn't it about time that you too repented and turned the controls over to the Lord? How long will you stubbornly persist in refusing God's help? On the outside you may even be a radiant Christian, but inside you know full well that you have developed a talent for putting on a pretty facade. God stands ready to fulfill your inner longing today!

It is as true for us as it was for the Ninevites that

A GODLY CHANGE OF MIND WILL PRODUCE A GODLY CHARACTER OF LIFE.

Footnotes

1. A.T. Olmstead, *History of Assyria*, pp. 169-174, as cited in Leon Wood, *A Survey of Israel's History* (Grand Rapids: Zondervan, 1970), p. 327.
2. E.B. Pusey, "Jonah" in *Barnes on the Old Testament, The Minor Prophets a Commentary*, vol. 1 (Grand Rapids: Baker Book House, 1973), p. 382.
3. Bruce Narramore and Bill Counts, *Guilt and Freedom* (Irvine, California: Harvest House Publishers, Inc., 1974), see the helpful comments in chapter 10, pp. 94-106.
4. The Hebrew word is *harah* and is used in Jonah 4:1,4,9. The root of the word means to cause a fire or a burning sensation.

12 | What Do You Say to an Angry Man?
Jonah 4:1–5

Our appointment had been set for 11:00 A.M. on Saturday morning. The time was clearly understood and the meeting place was to be at our apartment. When Saturday morning came Lynn and I got up early, had breakfast with Matthew, and then threw a few toys into the closet, dusted the furniture, and tidied up. You know the routine—it's the same at your home!

Finally 11:00 A.M. came. We heard no knock at the door, nor did we see any strange car pull up in front of the building. 11:30—12:00 noon, and still no visitor. About this time we began wondering if anything had happened to him. Lateness can certainly bring gruesome thoughts to one's mind!

Perhaps he was delayed at his previous appointment. Anyway, we decided to go ahead with lunch, half-expecting our friend to pop in the door at any moment.

12:30—1:00 P.M. Where in the world was he? The tension in the air began to mount at lunchtime; we were beginning to feel that the whole day was lost just waiting around.

He never came at all! Nor did he call or send a note. It wasn't until a week later that I heard a sheepish voice at the other end of the line say, "Well, Jim, I'm sorry, I got held up at the Bible College over some details relating to my ministry —and I just didn't get over to your place."

Though outwardly calm, inside I hit the boiling point; my blood almost churned as it gushed through my angry body! My reaction to a missed appointment with a Christian brother completely controlled my emotions—I was furious all day, all week Lynn saw it, and Matthew certainly noticed it in the way I talked with him.

What could my family say? What do you say to an angry man?

It took a good two weeks for me to settle down. That response had been so unlike my usual style that it really scared me. When we take a look at Jonah 4:1 the words are rather frightening indeed. I didn't expect anything like this!

What does God have for us in these opening sentences of Jonah 4? The obvious point is one that we desperately need: *The heat of anger can be cooled by recognizing God's love for all men.*

What's the Matter, Jonah?

After the tremendous transforming power of God had turned the city of Nineveh inside out, we might expect to hear an excited "Amen!" from brother Jonah. Instead we read, "But it greatly displeased Jonah, and he became angry" (4:1).

That's what the text says: Jonah was disgusted. Perhaps there is a textual problem here, and this is not really a part of the inspired canon? No, we can't avoid these words; they belong right here.

What's the matter, Jonah? Cheer up, look what God has done through you to His glory! But nothing was about to budge the angry prophet. The words literally describe the fact that he was red hot with anger. He was boiling mad![1]

Why was this successful preacher all bent out of shape? Jonah had repented and had been thoroughly disciplined in the Lord's special "school of discipleship" in the interior of the great fish, but apparently the heart of the prophet was still in the adjustment stages.

Jonah had changed his attitude about his selfish desires and had submitted to the word of the Lord, but now he was totally unprepared for the outcome! To see before his eyes the great repentance of these Gentile people in turning from their sins and calling out to Yahweh was too much. This was not supposed to happen!

Jonah's notebook did not contain a contingency plan for

133

the sweeping revival that was taking place. In his own finite mind he was still thinking that surely God's judgment would bring destruction on the city and that Israel would see this as a sign to wake up out of her own sinful ways.

"But, Lord, what happened? They're turning to you! Look at them—they're really changing! And now you're not going to bring the calamity on them which you promised." In the aftermath of one of the great moments in history, Jonah battled against the Lord's will.

While Nineveh was being transformed, Jonah was being tormented. Ecclesiastes 7:9 cautions us about the anger of the human heart: "Do not be eager in your heart to be angry, for anger resides in the bosom of fools."

How Do We Handle Anger?

How can we cool the flame of our hot emotions?[2] Let's look at two brief suggestions.

1. *Pinpoint the Cause.* When we really put our finger on the underlying cause of our anger, we may find an *improper view of God.* This was Jonah's problem at this point. He was blind to the all-encompassing love of God for others, including these Gentiles. He was totally fogged out in this area and saw only a limited view of the Lord.

Perhaps we may have an *inflated view of ourselves.* This is such a tempting snare for all of us. Paul cautions the believer "not to think more highly of himself than he ought to think; but to think so as to have sound judgment, as God has allotted to each a measure of faith" (Rom. 12:3). Jonah could have easily gotten a swelled head in seeing such an overwhelming response to the message he declared. Inflation is not just limited to the financial arena, but is also a deadly foe in the ego department!

Another cause may be an *incomplete view of others* and the needs in their lives. This was something that Jonah had some real problems with, and that same danger is inherent in any cross-cultural exposure. Superiority and aloofness can deafen a listening ear just as effectively as a wad of cotton!

Is the cause vertical? Am I angry and thrashing out at God?

Is the cause horizontal? Am I disappointed in myself or in others? Do I feel that I've received the short end of the stick and that the circumstances are unfair? Once the cause is located we need to move on to the next step.

2. *Prescribe the Cure.* The emphasis of this principle should be preventive rather than curative. But once the flame of anger has been kindled a cure is needed. What if you are mad at God? The solution may lie in the ignorance of His Word, the Bible. You may not be aware of the extent of His sovereign purposes. His gracious love is so attractive, but you may not know anything at all about His justice.

God is holy (see Isa. 6:3). He is absolute perfection. He does not show partiality to any mortal, but is perfectly gracious and just with every creature. Do you realize that He loves you no more and no less than He loved Moses? His love is consistent; it doesn't take sides. He loves you not because you are white or black or because you are a moral person, but because God *is* love (1 John 4:8,16)!

God is not just the white man's Lord, not just the clean-living people's God, nor just the God of the gross sinner. He is the God of *all* men and of *all* creation. Perhaps we stumble here, as Jonah did. The cure for this is to see the immensity of the Person of God! *The heat of anger can be cooled by recognizing God's love for all men.*

Here is an assignment that you can incorporate into your own personal devotions. Meditate on those portions of Scripture that describe the character of God. The chart, Diagram 10 is a starter:

Meditating on the Character of God

ATTRIBUTE	SCRIPTURE
His Self-existence	John 5:26; Ps. 94:8ff; Isa. 40:18; Rom. 9:19.
His Immutability	Ps. 33:11; Mal. 3:6; Heb. 13:8; Jas. 1:17.
His Infinity	Jer. 32:27; Ps. 40:5.
His Perfection	Job 11:7-10; Deut. 32:4.
His Eternity	Ps. 90:2; 2 Pet. 3:8; Heb. 1:2.

His Omnipresence	Ps. 139:7-9; Jer. 23:23,24; Eph. 4:6.
His Wisdom	Rom. 11:33; Prov. 8.
His Knowledge	Heb. 4:13; Isa. 40:13,14.
His Faithfulness	Lam. 3:22,23; 2 Tim. 2:13.
His Goodness	Matt. 5:45; Ps. 145:9.
His Love	Rom. 5:8; 1 John 3:1.
His Grace	2 Cor. 1:3; Ps. 86:5; Luke 1:50.
His Holiness	Exod. 15:11; 1 Sam. 2:2; Ps. 22:3; 1 Pet. 1:14-16.
His Sovereignty	Rom. 9:18; Eph. 1:11.

Complimentary Versus Critical

If you are down on yourself for your forgetfulness or your overeating or your lack of personal discipline, take heart! Have you ever realized that God has given you strengths as well? Maybe you need to discover that. Maybe we need to begin talking to one another more often with a complimentary tone rather than a critical spirit!

Perhaps we're saying, "When are you ever going to change?" "When will you ever wake up and get with it?" or, "Do you realize I've been married to you for over 10 years and all you've done is get worse?" If this is what we're saying, it's high time that we drastically alter our frame of appreciation.

Words like these leave deep, gaping wounds in our personalities. Even Avon's best cosmetic can't cover up those scars!

Have you seriously considered what a complimentary, encouraging attitude will produce? Try it. Experiment by starting right where you live and complimenting *everything* that is commendable! Try walking up to your sweetheart and beginning a conversation with the phrase, "Do you know what's so fantastic about your life?" And then tell him (or her) something great, no matter how insignificant you think it is. You may have to revive him if he passes out, but it will be worth it!

Anger can quickly develop into a first-class case of the

critical spirit. When that happens, a person's words become like drops of lethal poison pumped into a community water system—everyone around gets infected!

James, the half-brother of the Lord Jesus, gives us some practical admonition on this. We are to be "quick to hear, slow to speak and slow to anger" (Jas. 1:19; see also Prov. 15:18; 16:32; 14:29). Everything gets jumbled up and confused when the blast of heated anger goes uncontrolled. Slow down! Let the steam ooze out slowly; don't keep it bottled up until the pressure is ready to explode. If you're right at the bursting point, quickly get into a room by yourself and yell at the wall or into the air. Whatever you do, don't blast the nearest person who wanders by! A wall will not be damaged or threatened, but a person can be crippled with hurt.

Then take your Bible and open it to 1 Thessalonians 5:11. This is one of those surprising little verses that seem to stay tucked away from sight until they are really needed. What a great verse this is! "Therefore *encourage* one another and *build up* one another" (italics added).

The Praying Prophet
How did Jonah deal with his burning emotion? "And he prayed to the Lord" (4:2). Can you believe this? Jonah starts to pray! I wonder what kind of prayer this was. "And [he] said, 'Please Lord, was not this what I said while I was still in my own country? Therefore, in order to forestall this I fled to Tarshish, for I knew that Thou art a gracious and compassionate God, slow to anger and abundant in lovingkindness, and One who relents concerning calamity.' "

In the beginning of chapter 2, Jonah prayed with a thankful heart from the belly of the great fish. In the beginning of chapter 4, Jonah prays with a troubled heart from the city of Nineveh.

From a hot heart come hot words (see Prov. 15:1,2; 29:22; 30:33). The apostle Peter exhorts Christian husbands to "live with your wives in an understanding way, as with a weaker vessel, since she is a woman; and grant her honor as a fellow-heir of the grace of life, so that your prayers may not be

137

hindered" (1 Pet. 3:7). How words can fan the fires of conflict and tension, even between a man and his wife! Such a lack of understanding can seriously hinder one's prayer life.

Have you ever tried to talk with God when you're hot under the collar? Jonah did. Let's look at his prayer. "Please Lord." He begins with an entreaty to Yahweh. "Was not this what I said while I was still in my own country?" This sounds rather pompous! Jonah is quick to inform an omniscient God that he had told Him about what would happen while still in Israel.

"Remember, Lord, when I was talking with you, before I fled from your presence, before I took off for Joppa to go to Tarshish, I was discussing with you how this would all turn out." I wonder if Jonah really thought he was adding to the Lord's wealth of knowledge!

Then he said, "Therefore, in order to forestall this I fled to Tarshish." This is the most unbelievable prayer in the entire Bible. What a nearsighted view of God! What a twisted, distorted, incomplete perspective!

Jonah prayed as if God needed someone to help Him out, as if disobedience would help fulfill His sovereign plan! The real motives in Jonah's heart are now beginning to surface.

Jonah adds, "For I knew that Thou art a gracious and compassionate God, slow to anger and abundant in lovingkindness, and One who relents concerning calamity." Jonah had forecast the results because he knew what God was like. He mentions the attributes of God. He says he knows God's nature, but I wonder if he really grasped what he was saying. He listed the Lord's gracious characteristics—His compassion, His abundant lovingkindness—but Jonah's prayer unveiled the fact that much of his spirituality was just words! Above all, he had failed miserably to comprehend the loyal, covenant love of God for His own people. Much of Jonah's prayer was but an angry explosion of self-centered carnality.

Are We Just Spouting Off?

When we say, "Lord, I know you are kind, I know you are patient, I know you are forgiving, I know you will provide for my needs, I know you are powerful, I know you know everything there is or ever will be," do we really believe these words? Are these just correct biblical words, or have they penetrated our inner beings?

"Professors and not possessors." That's the phrase. We profess to know God in an intimate way, but how little of His nature is our possession! We pride ourselves in knowing much about God, but we're totally bankrupt in our personal relationship with Him.

The challenge before us is to correct our self-deceptive philosophy of the Christian life. In many ways the church of Jesus Christ, the living body of believers, has adopted this deceiving approach. Deep inside we think, "The more we accumulate, the better we'll be!" The sad result is what Dr. Grant Howard has termed "spiritual indigestion." Christians have been stuffed full of conferences, seminars, do-it-yourself notebooks, special classes, and home Bible studies; but instead of growing into the very image of Christ, we're lounging around in our comfortable cathedrals and giving off theological burps! Assimilation, not accumulation—that's the great need of our time! *Intense accumulation does not guarantee intimate acquaintance.*

The Lord Jesus spoke to this point in His message on the mount in Matthew chapters 5—7. "Many will say to Me on that day, 'Lord, Lord, did we not prophesy in Your name, and in Your name cast out demons, and in Your name perform many miracles?' And then I will declare to them, 'I never knew you; depart from Me, you who practice lawlessness' " (Matt. 7:22,23). Following this statement, Jesus told the story of the two builders. The thrust of the lesson was not how to build a beach house but how to build a life that will have lasting character. Such a life *assimilates* and *applies* the Word of God. The foolish man in Christ's story accumulated the right materials but failed to properly apply the truth. The end result was bitter indeed!

The Pleading Prophet
Maybe it was dawning on the angry prophet that he had a

great deal of head knowledge but very little character development. He knew the attributes of God, but the glory of it all had not been transferred down into the fabric of his life.

Listen as he continues his plea: "Therefore now, O Lord, please take my life from me, for death is better to me than life" (4:3). This is beginning to sound like a melancholy soap opera. I can almost hear the violins playing in the background! The irony of it all was that Jonah was dead serious. Moses had prayed like this (see Num. 11:15) and so had Elijah in his flight from Jezebel (1 Kings 19:4). Jonah was unwilling to take his own life because he knew that it was a sacred trust from Elohim. So he pleaded with the Lord to take it from him. When the apostle Paul said, "For to me, to live is Christ, and to die is gain" (Phil. 1:21), he was not struggling with improper motives. The heartrending decision that faced the apostle was whether to depart and be with his blessed Lord or to remain on in ministry to others. Paul was trying to discern between the better and the best!

Are you tempted to quit, to throw in the towel? Are you mad at God, even to the point of seeking an early out? Death is no escape from the responsibilities of life. If you feel you are pressed to the wall, remember the words in 1 Corinthians 10:13: "No temptation has overtaken you but such as is common to man; and God is faithful, who will not allow you to be tempted beyond what you are able; but with the temptation will provide the way of escape also, that you may be able to endure it."

The Penetrating God

The best method of dealing with an angry person is to respond in a soft, gentle manner. "A gentle answer turns away wrath, but a harsh word stirs up anger" (Prov. 15:1). God could have severely whipped Jonah into shape at this point, but He didn't. He asked of His servant a most penetrating question. "And the Lord said, 'Do you have good reason to be angry?' " (4:4).

Whenever I have been emotionally upset about a particular situation (and it seems to happen when least expected), it is those softly spoken, thought-provoking responses of Lynn that cut through the most. "Honey, have you the right to feel this way? Is this fair?"

God's statement to Jonah got right to the core of the problem! The Lord always gives tender counsel. He convicts without crushing. In this dialogue there is a fine point of application. Am I willing to allow God to ask me the same question? "What is your reason for acting like this? Is that right in My sight?"

If we were willing to permit God to pose that question in reference to our personal behavior, much of our living would be totally overhauled! Whenever we launch out into an area of sin, are we willing to hear the Lord's question? We are too quick to shut Him out; we don't really want Him to ask us because we are not willing to stop. God's grace should dilute the acid of our carnal desires.

Here's a home experiment you can try. The next time you encounter some mounting tension that begins to draw out some angry reactions, instead of popping your top or bringing the house down, *wait*! For a brief moment just try talking out loud, talking through that which is bugging you! Just wait, and talk. Don't scream, or yell, or fuss—just begin talking about the disturbing cause. Wait—and talk. Try it!

The Pondering Prophet

"Then Jonah went out from the city and sat east of it. There he made a shelter for himself and sat under it in the shade until he could see what would happen in the city" (4:5). Jonah could not stand it any longer, so he left the city. He had come in from the west, but now he goes out the "back door" toward the east. He deserts the very place where he should have stayed! The reluctant preacher is in no way interested in a follow-up program; he resorts to the "repent-and-run" technique or the "save-'em-and-leave-'em" tactic!

God never turned away from Jonah, but the prophet turns aside from the people. True, he did deliver God's message as he was commanded, but he fails here in a most essential task. What are the Ninevites to do now?

From the hill on the eastern bank of Nineveh Jonah had a bird's-eye view of the city. With the needs of the people shut out of his conscience, he engages in a construction project, assembling a Jewish booth, a tabernacle made of branches. Here was a product of Jonah's rebellious nature. God's heart was not controlling him, but only the burning disgust of his embittered emotions!

The shelter that Jonah made for himself was traditionally used in the celebration of the Feast of Tabernacles, or the Feast of Booths (see Lev. 23:33,34;cf. Exod. 23:16; Num. 29:12). This was Israel's final holiday. All the people were to live in these crude huts, something like a three-sided lean-to, for seven days (Lev. 23:39-44). This was one of the three feasts in Israel that required all the males to present themselves at the Temple in Jerusalem.

The Feast of Tabernacles was Israel's "Thanksgiving Day" as the people gave praise to Yahweh for the completion of the harvest. No servile work was to be performed as the people kept their year-end vows and were reminded of the Lord's sovereign care for their fathers in the wilderness.

This feast was not just a camp-out. Special burnt offerings were given. The typical significance of this event is seen in the fact that in the millennium, after Israel is regathered to the land and the national cleansing accomplished, there will be great millennial joy. The feasts of both Passover and Tabernacles will be observed during this millennial period.

So Jonah sat alone under his booth. One has written that "selfish ends and worldly devices are nothing more than booths in which men can never rest and find shelter." This kind of tabernacle was supposed to be a reminder of God's providential watch-care, but I'm sure Jonah wasn't thinking much about that. He was mad at God for showing such abundant mercy to his enemies!

The apostle Peter also wanted to go into the construction business while atop the Mount of Transfiguration (Matt. 17:1-9). The impetuous disciple said to Jesus, "We're having a great time up here, Lord! This is really fantastic! Let's build a few booths so we can stay longer with Moses and Elijah."

I imagine that in his excitement Peter thought Jesus was getting ready to bring in the millennium and to restore the kingdom to Israel (see Acts 1:6). Had he forgotten that Calvary still loomed ahead?

The Merciless Missionary

Jonah sat down when he should have been standing up; he retired in the shade when he should have been rejoicing in the sun! He waited to "see what would happen in the city." What was he expecting? Had there not been glorious repentance and turning to God? Yes, but Jonah was not waiting and watching for this.

Jonah sat in his ringside seat filled with pompous pride, a self-centered attitude, and a nearsighted view of the love of God. He was angry and stubborn. He waited until God's judgment would fall!

At this point the prophet had only one desire—for God's wrath to descend on the city. As he had pondered that brief message, "Yet forty days and Nineveh shall be overthrown," he must have thoroughly savored the judgment aspect; he had already shown his great surprise in the mercy aspect.

What Jonah needed to learn was that *the heat of anger can be cooled by recognizing God's love for all men.* The hot-blooded servant was determined to see God keep His promise and was prepared to stage a sit-down strike for the entire 40-day period until God kept His word.

As we leave this section we want to probe into our own lives. Are we doing this? Do we see only those favorite characteristics of God's nature, but blindly miss the rest? Are we hot and bothered and having a miserable experience in living the abundant life?

Who are we shutting out from receiving the blessings of God? How ridiculous it would be for me to preach the Word of God, call for a commitment to His truth, and then selfishly select those who could receive it! God loves even the Gentiles, even the neighbor next door who refuses to clean up his backyard, even that woman in your church who is loud and boisterous. God's viewpoint is inclusive, not exclusive!

Take a moment for a personal checkup. The following questions will serve as a diagnostic stethoscope for detecting the heartbeat of your own personal attitudes.

Personal Attitude	YES	NO	SOMETIMES
1. I feel some resentment toward certain people in our fellowship.	☐	☐	☐
2. My view of God is bigger than personal hang-ups.	☐	☐	☐
3. I know a lot *about* God, but feel that I really do not know Him personally.	☐	☐	☐
4. I can name at least one area in my life that has changed in the last three months.	☐	☐	☐
5. I am able to talk through my anger before exploding.	☐	☐	☐
6. I carefully avoid certain people so as not to greet them or talk with them below the surface level.	☐	☐	☐
7. I feel left out when others receive blessings and all I get are difficulties.	☐	☐	☐
8. I can name at least one sacrificial act I have done to help another person the last three months.	☐	☐	☐
9. When I want to quit or give up, it is usually because I am disappointed and hurt.	☐	☐	☐
10. I am willing to be used by God in loving my unlovely acquaintances.	☐	☐	☐

How did you do? If your negative answers tipped the scales, why not make these attitudes a number one priority in developing a walk "worthy of the calling with which you have been called, with all humility and gentleness, with patience, showing forbearance to one another in love, being diligent to preserve the unity of the Spirit in the bond of peace" (Eph. 4:1-3).

Along with Jonah, each of us needs to learn that

THE HEAT OF ANGER CAN BE COOLED BY RECOGNIZING GOD'S LOVE FOR ALL MEN.

Footnotes

1. See note 4, chapter 11.
2. See Colossians 3:8-10 and James 1:18-22.

13 | An Object Lesson That Cannot Be Refused
Jonah 4:6–11

The more I look at this man Jonah, the more I see of myself! This portion of Scripture is so real—it touches us right where we are living.

We have now come to the final chapter of this book and the concluding verses of Jonah's narrative. An angry old man is before our eyes. Our thoughts have been held captive as we have seen both the strengths and weaknesses of Jonah's character on the stage of life. We have watched him refuse the will of God and run in fear and disobedience; we have heard him respond to God's mercy and pray from "the depths of Sheol"; we have sat expectantly on the edges of our chairs as he obediently repeated the word of the Lord in the streets of Nineveh; and we have stood speechless as he voiced an angry prayer to the God who loved him.

God has the final word. He always does! The cantankerous, selfish Jonah is headed on a collision course with Almighty God. In this final encounter the Lord rebukes His servant, but not through the means of a great fish or a great storm, but through three common, insignificant things: a plant, a worm, and the east wind. God prepares for His prophet an object lesson that cannot be refused in driving home His final point: *selfishness is silenced by beholding the sovereignty of God.*

The Lord Prepares a Plant
"So the Lord God appointed a plant and it grew up over Jonah to be a shade over his head to deliver him from his discomfort" (4:6).

There he was, sitting in that crude, homemade hut and

pouting like a child! Jonah had prayed and pleaded to God in bitter disappointment over what had happened in the city, and now God has had it with Jonah.

Or has He? Look at verse 6. What's this? A plant to give Jonah more shade? Though Jonah resented God's sovereign mercy to the Ninevites, the Lord still continues to reach down and comfort His angry servant. Paul expressed this so beautifully in 2 Corinthians 1:3,4: "Blessed be the God and Father of our Lord Jesus Christ, the Father of mercies and God of all comfort; who comforts us in all our affliction so that we may be able to comfort those who are in any affliction with the comfort with which we ourselves are comforted by God."

Jonah's plant was "appointed" by God. Like the great storm and the great fish, this vegetable root was to be of great value in God's final object lesson. If you enjoy botany you will be pleased to know that this plant was in all probability a *Ricinus communis*, a castor-oil plant.[1] The Lord did not instantly create this plant, but He sovereignly used it in communicating His final lesson to a rebellious preacher. Researchers tell us that this plant can grow to a height of 10 feet, sometimes growing this tall in a matter of days. The broad green leaves of the plant provide welcome shade from the hot sun.

The text says "from his discomfort." Apparently the sun was not the only source of Jonah's heat; heat was also generated by Jonah's grumbling spirit! Physicians will verify the fact that emotional feelings need a proper outlet; if they are suppressed and allowed to build up, the human body may react violently in discomfort and sickness.

Jonah's positive response to this added protection is described as being "extremely happy." We enjoy the comforts of God's added blessings too! This scene is in vivid contrast to the terrifying storm on the sea, when even the sailors themselves were "extremely frightened" (1:10). In this short drama the full gamut of human emotions catches our attention.

While the troubled prophet is experiencing a temporary surge of happiness over a few leaves of shade, he is very unhappy about what is taking place in Nineveh. Here is the great irony of the human perspective: Man praises the insignificant and misses the truly significant. Another way of stating this is that men major on the minor issues of life.

The Lord Prepares a Worm

This tranquil scene was soon to be shattered by the entrance of another character in the drama. "But God appointed a worm when dawn came the next day, and it attacked the plant and it withered" (4:7).

First the storm, then the fish, then the plant, and now the worm![2] The plant provided shade for one day, but when the dawn came the following morning the plant was put out of commission. The worm's method of attack was probably achieved by chewing the roots under the soil. This was an inside job, and the plant literally dried up!

Have you noted the decreasing size of God's appointed servants? A *great* storm, a *great* fish, a *big* plant, and now a *small* worm. One person has written that "the worm of destruction gnaws the root of our best and most loved earthly joy." Let's look at two points of application that can be drawn from this incident.

1. *Our joys can be destroyed by little things.* Have you ever come home at night especially happy about your day at work or school? Perhaps you have received a word of encouragement and praise, or maybe even a promotion or raise! Everything has been just great, and you want to share this with your family. But before you have a chance to broadcast your joy, your wife lets you have it! That little comment, that subtle rebuke, that small reminder, and your balloon of happiness is quickly punctured! These "little" things happen more often than we care to admit.

2. *Our joys can be ruined by unseen things.* The worm probably ate the roots of the castor-oil plant; it nibbled away the source of its nourishment. The invisible worms of fear and worry and frustration can eat away at our personal joys too! But God is not finished yet. His third insignificant servant is ready to come on stage.

The Lord Prepares a Wind

"And it came about when the sun came up that God appointed a scorching east wind, and the sun beat down on Jonah's head so that he became faint and begged with all his soul to die, saying 'Death is better to me than life'" (4:8).

The term that Jonah employs in describing God's third envoy is literally "a scorcher." The Lord sent a scorching east wind, a "sirocco."[3] Volkswagen people have even named one of their VW import models the Sirocco, the "hot one." During my high school days our family moved to a new home on the banks of the Columbia River in Washington. The hot, dry climate in the eastern part of the state seemed always to reach into the 100-degree range every summer. Our home was poised over an embankment, and when the east winds blew they brought the unbearably blistering heat along with them. I remember being frustrated with that wind! You couldn't water-ski or play tennis or do anything! You could barely drive a car down the street without being blown off the road. I would ask, "Mom, what's the wind good for, anyway?"

I also recall my basic training days in Fort Polk, Louisiana. The sun poured down upon us like an open furnace. At several points the heat and winds were so sultry and sticky that we were allowed to train for only 15 minutes at a stretch.

Can't you just feel the sweat on Jonah's brow? There was his favorite plant now brown and withered, and the sun was his oppressive master.

The rays "beat down on Jonah's head." The same root word that is used in verse 7 to describe how the worm "attacked" the plant is employed here to indicate the burden of the hot sun. The heat was just as intense as Jonah's disgust! Jonah was on the verge of a sunstroke and he begged God to let him die. His mind was faint and reeling in this suffocating temperature: "Lord, take me home. Let me out of this place! Anywhere is better than being here. Death is better than life. I preached your word to those Gentile people, so now what's going to happen to Israel? Lord, even nature doesn't work for me. You seem to be allowing all of this to happen. Let me take the easy way out!"

149

The most insignificant item of all, the invisible wind, has brought the confused prophet to the end of the line. His thoughts are totally self-centered; all he sees is his own discomfort and pain. God must communicate to him the fact that *selfishness is silenced by beholding the sovereignty of God.*

God's Finale

As the Lord responds to His prophet the words nearly echo the reply in verse 4. "Then God said to Jonah, 'Do you have good reason to be angry about the plant?' And he said, 'I have good reason to be angry, even to death' " (4:9).

There is an additional phrase that God mentions here that was not included previously—"about the plant." The Lord had tried earlier to break through to the troubled Jonah, but to no avail. So now He directs His question toward the plant.

"Jonah, take a good, long look at that dried-up twig. Do you have any good reason to be acting the way you are toward that innocent plant?" There appears to be no pause in Jonah's cocky reply:

"Lord, you're darn right I'm angry, and I'm justified even to the point of dying!" Jonah maintains his ground and stubbornly refuses to let go of his selfish attitude.

The dialogue is over. With that last burst of pride, God begins His final remarks to the prophet.

"Then the Lord said, 'You had compassion on the plant for which you did not work, and which you did not cause to grow, which came up overnight and perished overnight' " (4:10).

This passage contains an exceptional chain of thought. From the insignificance of the plant, God focuses on the three most important realms of our existence. Let's notice what God is revealing to Jonah in this profound statement:

Birth—"The plant for which you did not work." You did not make the plant or produce it, Jonah. I gave it life. *Birth* begins with Me.

Life—"And which you did not cause to grow." You did not water it or care for it. I sustained its *life.*

150

Death—"Which came up overnight and perished overnight." All life is on My divine timetable. Nothing
dies without My knowledge.

In these comments about an insignificant castor-oil plant
on the eastern side of Nineveh, God opens up a vista that He
has never done before. God stuns Jonah's comprehension
with the great issues of *birth*, *life* and *death*! The object lesson
was clear: God is totally sovereign in every realm of existence.
He is the Creator, the Sustainer, and the Completer of all life.

God Is in Control

Just a brief time back I had the opportunity to officiate at
the graveside of a 30-day-old infant boy. As friends and rela-
tives of the young parents gathered under the awning, we read
the Word of God and prayed together.

I looked down at the little box. The flowers were so lovely;
the death was so tragic! God had created that little life, and
in His wisdom He took it back to Himself.

I kept staring at that little coffin. All that filled my heart
and mind was the overpowering sovereignty of the God that
loves us! Could any of us explain why this had happened? We
stood quietly in the cool breeze on that hillside meadow.

Inside my head was a stream of thoughts: "Lord, you are
in control. You are sovereign. You know why everything
happens and why everything comes to an end. I cannot grasp
how you operate. I don't know why you do the things you do,
but help me to trust you. Thank you, Father, that my life is
in your hands—every bit of it! You are the Lord!"

The Compassionate God

In verse 10 we have Yahweh ("the LORD") speaking. He is
the covenant-keeping God, the grace-manifesting God, the
One who exists in behalf of His own. We have the people on
the one hand and the plant on the other, the great and the
small, the significant and the insignificant; Yahweh is sovereign over all!

One final verse remains. The Lord did not need to utter another word to Jonah, but He does. After explaining His object lesson, God makes a clear application of its truth so that His prophet will not miss the point:

"And should I not have compassion on Nineveh, the great city in which there are more than 120,000 persons who do not know the difference between their right and left hand, as well as many animals?" (4:11).

The application comes in the form of a question. The Father's heart had looked upon the city and yearned in compassion. Such was the experience of the Lord Jesus as He looked over Jerusalem: "O Jerusalem, Jerusalem, who kills the prophets and stones those who are sent to her! How often I wanted to gather your children together, the way a hen gathers her chicks under her wings, and you were unwilling" (Matt. 23:37; cf. Luke 13:34,35).

God used an idiomatic expression in referring to the "120, 000 persons who do not know the difference between their right and left hand." This referred to the moral area, to those who were unable to discern between good and evil. The phrase marks out the number of those who were below the age of accountability. Thus, the Father saw 120,000 infants in need of His grace, and this great need had stirred His great heart!

Even the "many animals" (or "herds") contains an element of rebuke. Certainly Jonah belabored his grief over the plant to an excessive degree. Were not cattle and oxen more important than the plant? Calvin has said that "if Jonah was right in grieving over one withered shrub, it would surely be a harder and more cruel thing for so many innocent animals to perish."

"What could Jonah say to this? He was obliged to keep silence, defeated, as it were, by his own sentence" (Luther). Jonah sat there absolutely speechless. The sovereign compassion of God for all men had crushed him. He sat dumb in its glorious magnitude. No further word is recorded. There was nothing else to say. Jonah's *selfishness was silenced as he beheld the sovereign love of God!*

152

Greater than Jonah

The book of Jonah began with "the word of the Lord" coming to the prophet's ear; the book ends with the word of the Lord piercing the prophet's heart! In the book of Job we read, "Then the Lord answered Job and said, 'Will the fault-finder contend with the Almighty? Let him who reproves God answer it.' Then Job answered the Lord and said, 'Behold, I am insignificant; what can I reply to Thee? I lay my hand on my mouth' " (Job 40:1-4). And in the words of Agur, "If you have been foolish in exalting yourself or if you have plotted evil, put your hand on your mouth" (Prov. 30:32).

In the New Testament, the words of the Lord Jesus ring ever so clearly: "Then some of the scribes and Pharisees answered Him, saying, 'Teacher, we want to see a sign from You.' But He answered and said to them, 'An evil and adulterous generation craves for a sign; and yet no sign shall be given to it but the sign of Jonah the prophet; for just as Jonah was three days and three nights in the belly of the sea-monster; so shall the Son of Man be three days and three nights in the heart of the earth' " (Matt. 12:38-41).

Just how magnificent is our God? Listen to Paul's letter to the Colossians: "And He is the image of the invisible God, the first-born of all creation. For in Him all things were created, both in the heavens and on earth, visible and invisible, whether thrones or dominions or rulers or authorities—all things have been created through Him and for Him. And He is before all things, and in Him all things hold together. He is also head of the body, the church; and He is the beginning, the first-born from the dead; so that He Himself might come to have first place in everything. For it was the Father's good pleasure for all the fulness to dwell in Him, and through Him to reconcile all things to Himself, having made peace through the blood of His cross; through Him, I say, whether things on earth or things in heaven" (Col 1:15-20).

Thus it is that this great prophet of the Lord slips quietly away into the divine record of history. We do not know what finally happened to Jonah but we can imagine with some certainty that he learned the most significant truth in all of

153

life—the sovereign greatness and glory of God Himself!

What about *you*? Are you willing to learn this great "lesson." As you experience the joy of living in the will of God may you ever grow in your love for Him!

OUR SELFISHNESS IS SILENCED AS WE
BEHOLD THE SOVEREIGN LOVE OF GOD.

Footnotes

1. Ven T.T. Perowne, *Obadiah and Jonah* (Cambridge: University Press, 1905), p. 87.
2. The Hebrew word *tole'ah* usually describes a worm that destroys grapes and plants, devours corpses and symbolizes the weakness and insignificance of man. The word also occurs in Exodus 16:20; Deuteronomy 28:39; Job 25:6; Isaiah 41:14.
3. Pusey's notes in "Jonah" on the *sirocco* are interesting. "It [the sirocco] is greatly feared for its violence and relaxing qualities. Suffocating heat is a characteristic of these vehement winds. Even the well-seasoned Arab seeks shade during the day, and journeys by night" Pusey, "Jonah," in *Barnes on the Old Testament, The Minor Propehts a Commentary*, vol. 1 (Grand Rapids: Baker Book House, 1973), pp. 424,425.

How to Know the Will of God

The apostle John's emphasis of obedience to the will of God is significant: "And the world is passing away, and also its lusts; but the one who does the will of God abides forever" (1 John 2:17). Those living in fellowship ("walking in the light") with Christ will manifest two important attitudes:

1. A willing obedience toward the will of God;
2. An eternal perspective toward all of life.

True love for the Father will be evident as one obeys God from the heart. But *how* do we obey God? How do I really know what to do? Can I be sure of knowing God's will? These are important questions, and the Word of God gives us some helpful, practical answers!

I. What the Will of God Is Not

A. *It is not something God hides from us.* Our Father is not interested in keeping us guessing about His will. Study Hebrews 5:11-14. He delights in revealing His thoughts (1 Cor. 2:10–12).

B. *It is not necessarily hard, distasteful, or miserable.* Rather, the Lord's will is gracious, pure, and exciting! Obedience to His desires will yield personal satisfaction and joy!

C. *It is not only for mature, "professional" Christians.* Our God does not play favorites. Pastors, missionaries and Bible students have no special corner on God's will. It is universal and personal. *Each one of us* has a meaningful place in God's program!

D. *It is not just for "big" decisions.* How do you know if a "little" decision will not become something very important later on? *All* decisions we make are to be important in our walk with Jesus Christ!

E. *It is not related to any area of sin.* God is sovereign, even where sin is involved, but He will not lead us into any sin. Study James 1:13.

II. What the Will of God Is

A. *The will of God concerns our character.*

1. Our Sanctification: "For this is the will of God, your sanctification; that is, that you abstain from sexual immorality" (1 Thess. 4:3).

2. The Process of Sanctification: "But we all, with unveiled face beholding as in a mirror the glory of the Lord, are being transformed into the same image from glory to glory, just as from the Lord, the Spirit" (2 Cor. 3:18).

3. The Result of Sanctification: "And we know that God causes all things to work together for good to those who love God, to those who are called according to His purpose. For whom He foreknew, He also predestined to become conformed to the image of His Son, that He might be the first-born among many brethren" (Rom. 8:28,29).

B. *The will of God concerns individual service.* "For we are His workmanship, created in Christ Jesus for good works, which God prepared beforehand, that we should walk in them" (Eph. 2:10).

1. Two necessary foundation stones for every Christian:

   a. Salvation (John 1:12)
   b. Submission (Rom. 12:1,2)

2. Each believer has a unique life's journey:
   a. God promises guidance in this unique life's journey: "I will instruct you and teach you in the way which you should go; I will counsel you with My eye upon you" (Ps. 32:8).
   b. God provides guideposts along the way.
      1) The Word of God: "Thy word is a lamp to my feet, and a light to my path" (Ps. 119:105).
      2) The Holy Spirit: "But when He, the Spirit of truth, comes, He will guide you into all the truth; for He will not speak on His own initiative, but whatever He hears, He will speak; and He will disclose to you what is to come" (John 16:13).
      3) Prayer for wisdom: "But if any of you lacks wisdom, let him ask of God, who gives to all men generously and without reproach, and it will be given to him" (Jas. 1:5).
      4) A trustworthy Father: "Trust in the Lord with all your heart, and do not lean on your own understanding. In all your ways acknowledge Him, and He will make your paths straight" (Prov. 3:5,6).
      5) Counsel of concerned people: "Without consultation, plans are frustrated, but with many counselors they succeed" (Prov. 15:22).
      6) God-directed circumstances: "And Saul was in hearty agreement with putting him to death. . . . Therefore, those who had been scattered went about preaching the word. And Philip went down to the city of Samaria and began proclaiming Christ to them" (Acts 8:1,4,5).
      7) Peace of God: "And the work of righteousness will be peace, and the service of righteousness, quietness and confidence forever" (Isa. 32:17).

A flashlight will provide bright light for each immediate step, and it will also illumine a portion of the path ahead. Each time we step forward in the light a further section of our unique journey is made clear.

So it is with our gracious Father. We are not promised guidance far ahead, nor are we assured that we shall always know *how* God is going to work. But we are promised that God will guide and direct us as we make decisions along the way.

God's will is realized upon *every step*!

May He encourage you to keep on "[walking] in the light" (1 John 1:7).

Selective Bibliography

Alexander, Ralph H. *Class Notes.* Portland: Western Conservative Baptist Seminary, Spring 1974. Unpublished notes on *Jonah* from Hebrew 104.

Archer, Gleason L., Jr. *A Survey of Old Testament Introduction.* Chicago: Moody Press, 1964.

Blair, Allen J. *Living Obediently: Jonah.* New Jersey: Loizeaux Brothers, 1963.

Botterweck, G. Johannes, and Ringgren, Helmer, eds. *Theological Dictionary of the Old Testament,* vol. 2. Grand Rapids: Wm. B. Eerdmans, 1974.

Boyd, Robert T. *Tells, Tombs, and Treasures.* New York: Bonanza Books, 1969.

Brown, Francis; Driver, S.R.; and Briggs, Charles A., eds. *A Hebrew and English Lexicon of the Old Testament.* Oxford: Clarendon Press, 1974 reprint.

Bull, Geoffrey T. *The City and the Sign.* Grand Rapids: Baker Book House, 1970.

Bullinger, E.W. *Figures of Speech Used in the Bible.* Grand Rapids: Baker Book House, 1968 reprint.

Counts, Bill, and Narramore, Bruce. *Guilt and Freedom.* Santa Ana, California: Harvest House Publishers, 1974.

Delitzsch, F., and Keil, C.F. "Jonah" in *Minor Prophets* Commentary on the Old Testament, vol. 10. Grand Rapids: Wm. B. Eerdmans, 1971, reprint.

Ellisen, Stanley A. *Bible Workbook: Jonah.* Portland: Western Baptist Press, 1969.

Ellul, Jacques. *The Judgment of Jonah.* Grand Rapids: Wm. B. Eerdmans, 1971.

Feinberg, Charles Lee. *Jonah, Micah and Nahum.* New York: American Board of Missions to the Jews, 1951.

Gaebelein, A.C. *The Annotated Bible.* New Jersey: Loizeaux Brothers, 1970.

Gaebelein, Frank E. *The Servant and the Dove.* New York: Our Hope Press, 1946.

Girdlestone, Robert Baker. *Synonyms of the Old Testament.* Grand Rapids: Wm. B. Eerdmans, 1974 reprint.

Livingston, G. Herbert. "Jonah" in the *Wycliffe Bible Commentary.* Chicago: Moody Press, 1962.

MacLaren, Alexander. *Expositions of Holy Scripture,* vols. 3, 6. Grand Rapids: Wm. B. Eerdmans, 1942.

Martin, Hugh. *The Prophet Jonah.* London: Banner of Truth Trust, 1966.

McGee, J. Vernon. *Jonah, Dead or Alive?* Los Angeles: Church of the Open Door, n.d.

Orr, James, ed. *The International Standard Bible Encyclopaedia.* vols. 3, 4. Grand Rapids: Wm. B. Eerdmans, 1939.

Perowne, Ven. T.T. *Obadiah and Jonah.* Cambridge: University Press, 1905.

Pusey, E.B. "Jonah" in *Barnes on the Old Testament, The Minor Prophets a Commentary,* vol. 1 Grand Rapids: Baker Book House, 1973.

Roberts, Jim. *Poor Jonah.* St. Louis: Concordia Publishing House, n.d.

Robinson, George L. *The Twelve Minor Prophets.* Grand Rapids: Baker Book House, 1974 reprint.

Snaith, Norman H. *Notes on the Hebrew Text of Jonah.* London: The Epworth Press, 1945.

Trench, Richard Chenevix. *Synonyms of the New Testament.* Grand Rapids: Wm. B. Eerdmans, 1975 reprint.

Unger, Merrill F. *Introductory Guide to the Old Testament.* Grand Rapids: Zondervan, 1951.

Unger, Merrill F. *Unger's Bible Dictionary.* Chicago: Moody Press, 1967.

Wolfendale, James. *The Preachers Homiletic Commentary.* New York: Funk and Wagnalls Co., 1892.

Wood, Leon. *A Survey of Israel's History.* Grand Rapids: Zondervan, 1970.

Young, Edward J. *An Introduction to the Old Testament.* Grand Rapids: Wm. B. Eerdmans, 1949.